Cambridge Elements

Elements in Global China
edited by
Ching Kwan Lee
University of California-Los Angeles

CHINA AND THE GLOBAL ECONOMIC ORDER

Gregory T. Chin
York University, Canada

Kevin P. Gallagher
Boston University

Shaftesbury Road, Cambridge CB2 8EA, United Kingdom

One Liberty Plaza, 20th Floor, New York, NY 10006, USA

477 Williamstown Road, Port Melbourne, VIC 3207, Australia

314–321, 3rd Floor, Plot 3, Splendor Forum, Jasola District Centre, New Delhi – 110025, India

103 Penang Road, #05–06/07, Visioncrest Commercial, Singapore 238467

Cambridge University Press is part of Cambridge University Press & Assessment, a department of the University of Cambridge.

We share the University's mission to contribute to society through the pursuit of education, learning and research at the highest international levels of excellence.

www.cambridge.org
Information on this title: www.cambridge.org/9781009509084

DOI: 10.1017/9781009509053

© Gregory T. Chin and Kevin P. Gallagher 2025

This publication is in copyright. Subject to statutory exception and to the provisions of relevant collective licensing agreements, with the exception of the Creative Commons version the link for which is provided below, no reproduction of any part may take place without the written permission of Cambridge University Press & Assessment.

An online version of this work is published at doi.org/10.1017/9781009509053 under a Creative Commons Open Access license CC-BY-NC 4.0 which permits re-use, distribution and reproduction in any medium for non-commercial purposes providing appropriate credit to the original work is given and any changes made are indicated. To view a copy of this license visit https://creativecommons.org/licenses/by-nc/4.0

When citing this work, please include a reference to the DOI 10.1017/9781009509053

First published 2025

A catalogue record for this publication is available from the British Library

ISBN 978-1-009-50908-4 Hardback
ISBN 978-1-009-50907-7 Paperback
ISSN 2632-7341 (online)
ISSN 2632-7333 (print)

Cambridge University Press & Assessment has no responsibility for the persistence or accuracy of URLs for external or third-party internet websites referred to in this publication and does not guarantee that any content on such websites is, or will remain, accurate or appropriate.

For EU product safety concerns, contact us at Calle de José Abascal, 56, 1°, 28003 Madrid, Spain, or email eugpsr@cambridge.org

China and the Global Economic Order

Elements in Global China

DOI: 10.1017/9781009509053
First published online: October 2025

Gregory T. Chin
York University, Canada

Kevin P. Gallagher
Boston University

Author for correspondence: Gregory T. Chin, gtchin@yorku.ca

Abstract: This Element examines China's evolving relations with the Bretton Woods institutions (BWIs), specifically the International Monetary Fund and the World Bank Group from the 1980s through 2025. Using a combination of new qualitative findings and quantitative datasets, the authors observe that China has taken an evolving approach to the BWIs in order to achieve its multiple agendas, acting largely as a "rule-taker" during its first two decades as a member, but, over time, also becoming a "rule-shaker" inside the BWIs, and ultimately a new "rule-maker" outside of the BWIs. The analysis highlights China's exercise of "two-way countervailing power" with one foot inside the BWIs, and another outside, and pushing for changes in both directions. China's interventions have resulted in BWs reforms and the gradual transformation of the global order, while also generating counter-reactions especially from the United States. This title is also available as Open Access on Cambridge Core.

This Element also has a video abstract:
www.Cambridge.org/EGLC-Chin_abstract

Keywords: China, United States, BRICS, global economic order, Bretton Woods, International Monetary Fund, World Bank

© Gregory T. Chin and Kevin P. Gallagher 2025

ISBNs: 9781009509084 (HB), 9781009509077 (PB), 9781009509053 (OC)
ISSNs: 2632-7341 (online), 2632-7333 (print)

Contents

1 China and the Evolution of the Global Economic Order   1

2 How China Remakes the Global Monetary System   15

3 How China Remakes Global Development Finance   38

4 China and the Future of the Bretton Woods Order   60

   References   66

1 China and the Evolution of the Global Economic Order

China's rise has given new momentum to the decades-long calls from across the Global South for a more balanced world economic order. In October 2024, the expanded Brazil, Russia, India, China, and South Africa (BRICS) coalition, now significantly larger than the economies of the Group of 7 (G7), met to build alternatives to the World Bank (WB), the International Monetary Fund (IMF), and international payment systems, and to reform the Western-led 'legacy' institutions. A month earlier, fifty heads of African states traveled to Beijing to seek financing for infrastructure and clean energy from China's two global 'policy banks', the China Development Bank and the State Export-Import Bank of China. A year before, China hosted the tenth anniversary of its Belt and Road Initiative (BRI), celebrating the over US$1 trillion invested in the Global South and Europe, and committed to a new wave of investment, especially for green development. Heads of state in attendance from across the Global South, along with the United Nations (UN) Secretary-General, applauded the BRI and collectively called for deeper reforms of the global economic order.

This Element traces the role of China in re-making the rules, norms, authority patterns, and institutional arrangements that make up the established Bretton Woods system. The analysis highlights China's role in establishing key elements of an extended transition or transformation to the emerging global economic order.[1] Our analytical starting point is that we are in the interregnum phase of an extended period of world order change, which is giving rise to a new global economic order that entails either a fundamental remaking of the Bretton Woods system or even more profound changes that can be called 'post-Bretton Woods'. By 'rules', we mean explicit, formal, legally binding arrangements, whereas we understand 'norms' as implicit, widely shared expectations about appropriate behavior, though not legally binding, such as voluntary codes of conduct or shared intersubjective understandings. Both rules and norms, especially when reinforced through institutions, are conceived as crucial for ordering behavior, social reality outcomes, and authority patterns in international organization (Finnemore and Sikkink, 1998; Barnett and Finnemore, 2004).

---

[1] The General Agreement on Tariffs and Trade (GATT) was also spawned at the Bretton Woods conference, with a hope for an 'International Trade Organization' that eventually led to the creation of the World Trade Organization (WTO) in 1994. The GATT-WTO is not included in this Element due to space constraints, and also because the global trade system was not complete for decades. However, the substantial published scholarship on China and the WTO indicates that China has exhibited similar hybrid behaviour in relation to the GATT/WTO, as well as creating regional or pan-regional trade agreements alongside or beneath the WTO, and has exercised two-way inside-outside leverage and influence. See: Pearson, 2006; Zeng and Liang, 2013; Hopwell, 2016; Shaffer and Gao, 2017; Gao, Reass and Ka, 2023.

We center on the Bretton Woods institutions (BWIs) forged at the UN Monetary and Financial Conference held in Bretton Woods, New Hampshire, in 1944, where the Allied representatives met to undertake the unprecedented endeavor of planning the international economic order (Frieden, 2019). The resulting BWIs – the dollar-gold standard, IMF, and WB – formed the core of the post-World War II global economic order that aimed to maintain peace through stable and shared growth and prosperity. At first, the Bretton Woods regime seemed to preside over two decades of robust world trade and growth with relative financial stability, though more so in higher-income economies. The system came under immense pressure at the end of the 1960s as the United States ran persistent current account deficits and exposed the limits of the IMF to manage the system of dollar-gold pegged exchange rates. In 1971, the United States suspended the convertibility of the dollar into gold and abandoned it in 1973 (Eichengreen, 2019).

As the dollar-gold standard and fixed exchange rate regime came to an end, the BWIs shifted from "embedded liberalism," whereby markets are embedded within rules and norms to promote stability, cooperation, full employment, and equity, to become the standard-bearers of "neo-liberalism" that favored the reduction of the state in economic affairs over more universal, private market-determined approaches to welfare. In the midst of this global policy and regulatory transformation, the People's Republic of China (PRC) assumed the seat of "China" at the IMF and the WB in 1980. China embarked on an extended period of market reforms and opening to the world economy during the 1980s and 1990s. China's membership in these institutions was largely beneficial for both China and the global economy. The BWIs cannot take full credit for China's growth miracle by any means, but they did provide substantial policy advice, technical assistance, and financing that supported China's economic reforms (Jacobson and Oksenberg, 1990; Hu 2004; Chin, 2012). The assistance from the IMF and WB in supporting China's growth and stability has proved indispensable for the West as well, as China's global integration provided new markets, lower priced goods, and increased channels for diplomatic exchange (Kastner, Pearson, and Rector, 2019).

In this twenty-first century, we are seeing the emergence of a less-centralized, more fragmented, and globally diverse system. The US dollar, capital markets, and central banks still occupy the core of the monetary and financial systems in the advanced economies, and the IMF continues to serve as the main lender of last resort for most lower-income countries. Middle-income countries have pushed back on the North-South asymmetry as they work to create parallel institutions and policy space to determine domestic policies. Chief among those present at the creation of these alternative institutions is China. Parallel to the evolution of the BWIs, China has established or co-established a number of international economic institutions that, cumulatively, have similar financial firepower and mirror the functions of the IMF and the WB. These institutions have spurred economic growth, provided emergency financing, and increased the agency of developing countries in international economic affairs.

In the realm of global development finance, China's two state policy banks – China Development Bank and the Export-Import Bank of China – have provided roughly the same amount of financing to developing countries during the same time period as the WB (2008–2022). China played a leading role in establishing two new Multilateral Development Banks (MDBs): the Asian Infrastructure Investment Bank (AIIB) and the BRICS-led New Development Bank (NDB). In the international monetary realm, China's central bank helped to build an "Asian regional financial safety net," known as the Chiang Mai Initiative Multilateralization (CMIM), and, since 2008, China has supported the growing international use of its national currency, the renminbi (RMB), for trade finance and emergency financial support. China has also provided accompanying RMB currency swap lines for trade financing and liquidity support and has built a Cross-border Interbank Payment System (CIPS) for direct cross-border settlement of transactions using RMB. This new infrastructure is analogous to the US dollar payments system, comprising the US Federal Reserve-owned Fedwire, the private sector counterpart Clearing House Interbank Payments System (CHIPS), and the Society for Worldwide Inter-bank Financial Telecommunication (SWIFT), headquartered in Belgium.

Eighty years after their founding, the BWIs are under intense scrutiny for their lackluster responses to the international financial crises of the mid- to late-1990s and 2007–09, as well as their limited ability to respond to the increased prevalence of climate change, growing sovereign debt distress, the persistence of global economic inequities, pandemic preparedness, and for the lack of voice and representation for the majority of the membership that resides in the Global South. Inside the corridors of the BWIs, there is growing awareness of the need to reform the IMF and WB. Some Western governments have come around to supporting the reform of the institutions, including the United States, which had the largest hand in creating the BWIs and in maintaining them.

How has China's role expanded inside the BWIs and outside? What are China's motivations, interests, and goals inside the BWIs and outside? How have the BWIs responded to China and further engaged with China, and why? What have been the motivations among the Western powers, and how have their responses evolved over time in relation to China's evolving behavior? Are Western governments motivated as enlightened hegemons, organically seeking to improve the provision of global public goods? Or are Western powers now seeing a growing "China threat" and competition from other Global South powers and pushing back? What is next?

Whereas earlier scholarship identified China largely as a **"rule taker"** *inside* the BWIs and accepting of the existing rules and established order, we argue that China has increasingly become a **"rule-maker,"** a creator of new rules, norms, and standards through the establishment of parallel institutions *outside* of the BWIs. This hybrid behavior has further enabled China to gain more influence as a **"rule shaker"** *inside* the BWIs. The hybrid positioning opens the door for China (and other Southern nations) to choose whether to remain engaged and pursue further reforms of the BWIs or focus instead on developing alternative rules, norms, and institutions *outside* the BWIs. Most countries in the Global South, so far, have tried to avoid making a binary choice between one or the other and have sought to benefit from engaging both inside and outside the BWIs. Through their hybrid efforts, China and other Southern nations are gradually bringing about transformational changes in the global economic order.

We see China's hybrid positioning as an exercise of two-way *countervailing power*. By creating alternative institutions and coalitions outside of the BWIs, China has presented a credible possibility of exit from the BWIs, while these outside activities also simultaneously pave the way for China or others to leverage the extra-forum activity to pressure for changes in the rules, norms, and standards back inside the IMF and WB. At times, this phenomenon has been a conscious objective, and at others, a result of an increasingly integrated co-evolution. And at times, countervailing monetary power has also resulted from the interventions of others, including the representatives of Western nations motivated by a strategy to keep China inside the BWIs.

The majority of the literature in the social sciences has also depicted China as playing an "inside-outside" game to the betterment of China, while the implications for the system as a whole are still debated (e.g. Shambaugh, 2013; Wang, 2018; Kastner, Pearson, and Rector 2020; Friedberg, 2022). However, the studies that have focused on China and the BWIs (Wang, 2018; Kastner, Pearson, and Rector, 2019; Malkin and Momani, 2019) have tended to argue that despite whatever alternative institutional arrangements that China has fostered, these outside efforts are largely about China exerting influence back into the Bretton Woods systems, and as such, are ultimately status quo-oriented. By conceptualizing the countervailing power instead as *two-way* leverage, we suggest instead that China is increasing its influence within the BWIs, providing functions similar to the BWIs, but also creating alternative non-BWs institutional options and policy space, and paving a potential off-ramp from the BWIs in the event the BWIs are deemed no longer fit for purpose. Finally, we emphasize that the outcome of China's exercise of hybrid positioning and two-way countervailing power is a gradual transformation towards a more balanced, multi-polar global economic order.

The Twentieth Century Global Economic Order

In his classic book, *The World in Depression*, economist and former statesman Charles Kindleberger argued that the Great Depression of 1929 spread from the United States to the rest of the world because the global community lacked a global leader and a set of rules that could provide five global public goods: a stable monetary and exchange rate system; a lender of last resort to provide liquidity to distressed nations; counter-cyclical and long-run public lending; open markets in recessions; and international policy coordination across these issues. Britain attempted a global economic conference in 1933 but failed to lead, as the rising United States also failed to step into the void. This interregnum triggered industrialized countries to erect trade barriers and implement beggar-thy-neighbor currency devaluations that drastically reduced international trade and foreign investment, hastening the global spread of the Great Depression and accentuating geopolitical tensions ahead of World War II.

It seemed, though, that the same mistake would not be made twice when, amid the great destruction of World War II, the United States hosted the 1944 UN Monetary and Financial Conference in Bretton Woods, New Hampshire (Helleiner, 2014a). US Treasury Secretary Henry Morgenthau, Jr., premised the negotiations on the notion that, "prosperity, like peace, is indivisible. We cannot afford to have it scattered here or there among the fortunate or to enjoy it at the expense of others. Poverty, wherever it exists, is menacing to us all and undermines the well-being of each of us. It can no more be localized than war, but spreads and saps the economic strength of all the more favored areas of the earth" (James, 2012, 413). Under this rubric, those gathered rejected a return to the classical liberal order of the gold standard and the League of Nations, which forced countries to "adjust" to international payment fluctuations through austerity. Instead, a new set of institutions was built under what was termed "embedded liberalism," whereby markets were rooted in domestic institutions geared toward promoting stable growth, social welfare, and full employment (Ruggie 1982; Helleiner, 1994; Eichengreen, 2019).

To this end, the cornerstone of the system that negotiators at Bretton Woods agreed upon was a fixed dollar-gold standard that allowed countries to deploy capital controls to provide insulation from external shocks and space for full employment policies, while also permitting countries to adjust their national currency-dollar-pegs in exceptional circumstances. Relatedly, the IMF was created to facilitate an orderly system of international payments at stable and adjustable exchange rates and regulated capital flows. Most importantly, the Fund was charged with providing short-term international liquidity to avoid deflationary adjustments and to maintain stable exchange rates during balance of payments shortages (Eichengreen, 2019). Under the Articles of Agreement that established the IMF, member states were assigned "quotas," which were roughly based on the country's share of international trade and gross domestic product (GDP). IMF quotas determined the amount of gold and dollars that each member had to contribute to the Fund, but also the relative amount of drawing and voting rights that a member could exercise.

The IMF was created to monitor the stability of the financial system and provide short-term liquidity support, whereas the International Bank for Reconstruction and Development (IBRD) was established to provide medium- to long-run post-war reconstruction and counter-cyclical development financing. It was commonly understood that the terms and conditions of private markets did not function in a counter-cyclical manner and that public investment was needed to repair war-torn Europe and later to raise living standards in developing countries. IBRD member countries contribute (paid-in and callable) capital roughly commensurate to their trade and GDP, determining their relative levels of voting power. This base capital is used as collateral to tap capital markets and on-lend to borrowing member states at cheaper rates (Humphrey, 2022). The IBRD has since evolved into a "World Bank Group" that includes the IBRD (non-concessional financing), the International Development Association (IDA, highly concessional loans and grants), the International Finance Corporation (equity), the Multilateral Investment Guarantee Agency, and the International Center for the Settlement of Investment Disputes.

In addition to the economic and security rationale for establishing the BWIs, scholars have argued that negotiators also sought to correct governance failures at the global level. Kindleberger attributes the failure of the 1933 World Economic Conference in London to the decline of British hegemony (Kindleberger, 1973). By linking the fixed but adjustable gold standard to the United States dollar, and through the effective veto power derived from the quota and capital/voting system of the IMF and the IBRD, the Bretton Woods order essentially made the United States, and later the West, the hegemons of systemic stability in charge of the provision of international public goods. Later known as "hegemonic stability theory," the idea was challenged by scholars within the Liberal Institutionalist canon, who argued that as long as members (including new members such as China) collectively adhered to the norms and rules of the system, a hegemon may not be necessary for the maintenance of the order, what political scientists refer to as "regime theory" (Keohane, 1984).

More critical scholars saw the same period as the making of the post-World War II US-centered hegemonic world order, combining the exercise of consensus (public goods provision) and coercion (military power), or structural power. Some have seen US hegemony as in crisis from the early 1970s onward, whereas others see the continuation of US dominance based on its assertion of inter-related structures of power (Cox, 1987; Gilpin, 1987; Strange, 1987).

In the late-1940s and 1950s, the BWIs were primarily focused on the industrialized world but became more "global" in their institutional reach as former colonies gained independence and as the Cold War thawed in the 1990s. The period between the 1980s and the late 2000s is generally considered the era of "neo-liberalism" and the "Washington Consensus." Since then, a debate has emerged between those who argue that US and Western hegemony has continued and those who see the world order as shifting toward a more pluralistic, diverse, fragmented, or multipolar order (Helleiner, 2014; Drezner, 2014; Jones, 2014; Alden and Vieira, 2005; Barma, Ratner, and Weber, 2007; Drezner, 2007a; Cox, 2002; Ikenberry and Inoguchi, 2007; Cohen, 2008). Scholars who argue the latter perceive a diminution of US power and leadership and less widely accepted norms, rules, and institutions amid a greater mix of national and regional powers, more diverse sources of norms and influences, and corporate or societal actors, forming a less-centralized, more negotiated, messier, multi-centered world economic order (Kissinger, 2010; Bremmer, 2012; Kupchan, 2012; Kirshner, 2014; Acharya, 2017; Layne, 2018).

Since its onset in 1944, the Bretton Woods order has been evolving. The fiat US dollar still stands at the top of the global monetary pyramid, flexible exchange rates of varying degrees remain the norm, and international capital markets are the source of liquidity for most, except the poorest countries. From a multilateral perspective, the IMF – as the only institution with a global membership charged with maintaining global financial stability and still the holder of the largest emergency financing capacity – remains at the center of what is now referred to as the "Global Financial Safety Net" (GFSN). However, we also observe the emergence of a more multi-tiered and diverse GFSN that includes central bank swaps, regional financial arrangements (RFAs), newer contingent reserve arrangements, such as the BRICS Contingent Reserve Arrangement (CRA), and national reserves. In terms of global development finance, the WB remains at the center of a system of MDBs that includes regional and inter-regional multilateral banks, which largely follow the WB financing and governance model. But we also see the emergence of newer self-styled "Southern development finance institutions" in the AIIB and NDB. National development banks and state policy banks also lend more internationally than the established MDBs. The Group of Twenty (G20), the resurrected

G7, and the BRICS Plus grouping have emerged as the main informal consultative forums for the management of the global economy. The new and reshaped rules, norms, standards, and principles of this emerging global economic order are still heavily contested, as is the balance between efficiency and equity, and the degree of commitment to environmental sustainability. But their emergence can be tracked.

China and the Bretton Woods Institutions

China played a role in the formation of the post-World War II global economic order, represented by the Republic of China (1912–1949) at the Bretton Woods (BW) conference in 1944, and the People's Republic of China (PRC, 1949 onward) has been a significant contributor since it officially assumed the seat of 'China' at the two main BWIs in 1980. The core strategic motive that has remained throughout China's involvement with the BWIs is to learn and obtain what it needs to pursue its own national economic development objectives, without wholesale assimilation to the norms of the institutional order. Beijing has repeatedly stated that it is not seeking to undo or supplant the global order, but to re-balance it (Lin, 1981; Gao, 2023). For example, Liu Jianchao, head of the Chinese Communist Party's (CCP) International Department, recently told a US-based audience at the Council on Foreign Relations that, "China does not seek to change the current international order, still less reinvent the wheel by creating a new international order. We are one of the builders of the current world order and have benefited from it." China's goal, he said, was to "deliver a better life for the Chinese people" (Liu, 2024).

Whether the PRC is behaving solely or largely as a status quo actor, or, on balance, is behaving more as a system transformer, deserves further scrutiny. We address this question first by categorizing China's related actions and the institutional outcomes as those *inside* the BWIs versus *outside* the BWIs. Next, we assess China's behavior inside and outside the BWIs, and the resulting outcomes, using the rubric of "rule-taker," "rule-maker," and "rule-shaker." We find that China is engaging in rule-making outside of the BWIs and rule-shaking inside the BWIs to such a degree that the rules and norms are being reshaped, and the global economic order is being incrementally transformed.

Table 1 provides a snapshot of the key moments of China's engagement with the Bretton Woods order; subsequent sections will delve into more detail in tracing China's evolving relations with each BWI institution. In the left-hand column, the table highlights the main elements of China's involvement "inside" the BWIs. The right-hand column illustrates China's major initiatives "outside" of the BWIs.

Table 1 Tracing China and the Bretton Woods Order

	Inside	Outside
1944	Republic of China delegation to Bretton Woods	
1949		PRC Founded
1950	PRC excluded from BWIs	
1955		Bandung Conference
1960	Tapei loses ED seat	
1964		G–77 founded
1971		PRC recognized at UN
1974		New International Economic Order formed
1978		Deng Xiaping Reforms launched
1980	PRC joins WB and IMF	
1989	WB suspends processing China loans	
1994		China Development Bank and Export Import Bank of China launched
1997	China calls for IMF reform due to Asian Financial Crisis	
1999	China graduates from IDA	
2000		Chang Mai Initiative Founded
2001		Shanghai Cooperation Corporation Founded
2002	China proposes SDRs as reserve currency	
2006	China echoes call for SDRs as reserve currency	
2007		
2008	First PRC WB Senior VP and Chief Economist	USD reserves in PBOC reach $1 trillion
2009	IMF SDR issuance	First BRICS summit, First PBOC swap line
2010	IMF quota increase	Chang Mai Initiative Multilateralization
2011	First PRC Deputy Managing Director, IMF	
2012	Institutional View on capital account	
2013		Belt Road Initiative launched

Table 1 (cont.)

	Inside	**Outside**
2014		AIIB, NDB/CRA established, Silk Road Fund Launched
2015		CIPS launched
2016	RMB incorporated in SDR basket; China Hosts G20	
2018	World Bank capital increase	
2020	DSSI, Common Framework Launched	
2021	IMF SDR issuance	
2022	World Bank Evolution launched, CAF	
2023		BRICS expansion, 10th anniversary of BRI

Source: Authors' compilation.

As the following sections will outline, the PRC's engagement and relationship with the IMF can be defined as "highly professional," though less convivial than with the World Bank. Jacobson and Oksenberg (1990) were the first to conduct a detailed analysis of China and the BWIs and concluded: "At least in the first decade of its unfolding, the initial inclusion of China into the keystone International Economic Institutions was successful, judged by the standards of both sides. By and large, China abided by the rules that other large developing countries accepted. Moreover, China made discernible contributions to the operations of the BWIs as well" (17). Inside the BWIs, China's "rule-taking" was and is manifested, first and foremost, by accepting the US dollar-denominated world economy. China's trade, investment, and even its development assistance loans as a recipient were largely conducted in dollars. China also accepted the IMF's surveillance activity and has internalized many of the IMF's policy lessons, norms, and standards into its macroeconomic management, as well as its fiscal and financial systems.

Nonetheless, from the outset of its membership, China did not support the Fund's policy conditionality that called for slashing government spending and reducing the role of the state in economic affairs – a position that became even more steadfast following the IMF's disastrous record during the Asian Financial Crisis (Jacobson and Oksenberg, 1990; Helleiner and Momani, 2014; Nolan, 2021). To avoid conditionality, China has only taken technical assistance loans from the IMF. Throughout its history, China has called for greater voice and representation of developing countries and reform of IMF conditionality. As a participant in coalitions with East Asian countries, and later the BRICS, the PRC played a key role in reforming rules such as a 2010 increase in quotas – and thus, voting power – for China and others, as well as the IMF's updated stance on capital account liberalization and capital controls in 2012 (Gallagher, 2015; Grabel, 2018; Roberts, Armijo, and Katada, 2018; Kastner, Pearson, and Rector, 2019). Since 2011, a PRC national has been appointed to a Deputy Managing Director position at the IMF. In addition to increasing quotas at the IMF, China has succeeded in being a voice for other rule changes, such as increasing the size of the GFSN through issuances of the IMF's reserve accounting tool, Special Drawing Rights (SDR), and for expanding the use of the SDR as a reserve management tool. On a number of occasions, China has gone so far as to call for an increased role for the SDR and a reduced role for the US dollar as the de facto global settlement and reserve currency (Chin, 2014; Helleiner and Momani, 2014). China also successfully lobbied the IMF membership for the RMB to be included in the SDR reserve basket in 2016 (Wang, 2018; Kastner, Pearson, and Rector, 2019). The United States has resisted increased use of SDR, seeing expanded use as a potential threat to dollar supremacy and US political objectives at the IMF.

In terms of global development finance, China's engagement inside the World Bank has been comparatively convivial, particularly during the 1980s and 1990s when China was "learning" the norms, rules, and standards of the World Bank and undergoing "socialization" (Jacobson and Oksenberg, 1990; Johnston, 2008). During its first-two decades as a member of the World Bank, China absorbed economic reform policy advice and lessons from pragmatic experts willing to work within the economic policy limits of China's Communist Party-state-led system, including maintaining a role for state companies while also supporting the growth of the private sector (Bottelier, 2007). During the 1980s and 1990s, China and the Bank co-produced numerous studies on economic reform that helped Chinese officials chart their own reform path, including future Premier Zhu Rongji. Moreover, China benefited from numerous World Bank (and Asian Development Bank) concessional loans before "graduating" from IDA in 1999.

Despite the rather warm relations, as we will show in our section on the World Bank and development finance, China has played a strong hand and succeeded in changing the Bank's norms and rules. For example, China was able to avoid adopting many of the "shock therapy" and "Washington Consensus" suite of rapid privatization and marketization policies that other developing countries had to accept to receive World Bank financing (Bottelier, 2007). Indeed, even as China was engaging constructively with the BWIs and has continued to "learn" and absorb from the BWIs, it has also taken part in efforts to reform the BWIs, constructed its own set of institutions, and joined other Southern-led coalitions to push for changes to the BWIs.

Starting in the late 1990s, China began to work outside the BWIs to address international monetary and global development finance needs that were largely unmet or left unaddressed by the BWIs and the Western powers. On the monetary front, working outside of the IMF, China co-founded the Chiang Mai Initiative in 2000, together with the ten ASEAN nations, Japan, and South Korea ("ASEAN+3"), to provide a regional emergency liquidity fund operated by and for East Asian member countries. ASEAN+3 boosted the reserve pool of the Chiang Mai Initiative in 2010 to $240 billion, and China, in turn, supported the creation of a similar "Contingent Reserve Arrangement" with the BRICS nations in 2014. What is more, like many of its East Asian counterparts, China has amassed large national foreign exchange reserves to self-insure and insulate itself from financial instability and reliance on the IMF. China's national reserves reached US$1 trillion in 2007, topped out at an unprecedented $4 trillion in 2014, and now stand at over US$3 trillion. China also began to support the growing international use ("internationalization") of its national currency, the renminbi (RMB), in 2008, creating and launching its own cross-border RMB direct payments system, the CIPS, in 2015. The new rules of these alternative institutional arrangements are detailed in Section 2.

Operating outside of the World Bank, China has also played a major role in expanding development financing globally. In 1994, China established the China Development Bank (CDB) and the Export-Import Bank of China (CHEXIM), mainly to provide domestic lending for the country's national development and concessional state policy-related trade financing, respectively. Two decades later, CDB and CHEXIM are among the largest development lenders in the world, and from 2010–2020, they provided more financing to developing countries than the World Bank. These two banks, alongside China's Silk Road Fund, are the flagship institutions for China's outbound development finance, including financing Belt and Road Initiative (BRI) projects, the ambitious pan-regional connectivity stratagem that China launched in 2013. These financial institutions, together with China's state commercial banks, have provided upwards of US$1 trillion in financing to BRI partner and developing countries.

Furthermore, China has helped establish two new MDBs: the BRICS-led NDB and the 109-member AIIB, launched in 2015 and 2016, respectively. In Table 1 and Table 2, we list the creation of AIIB and NDB as examples of China acting as a rule-maker outside the BWIs, as these alternative institutions exhibit a spectrum of new and existing rules and norms. Some of their other rules are almost the same as those of the Western-dominated BWIs, but with China at the

Table 2 China's countervailing power in the Bretton Woods System

	Monetary System	**Development Finance System**
Rule-Taker	US dollar IMF member Financial socialization	Legacy MDB member Socialized norms
Rule-Maker	RMB Internationalization PBOC liquidity swaps CDB liquidity loans CMIM/CRA	CDB/CHEXIM/Equity Funds AIIB/NDB Belt Road Initiative
Rule-Shaker	SDR issuances RMB in SDR basket IMF capital account policy IMF quota reform	Capital Increases/Voice reform Shift to infrastructure World Bank conditionality

Source: Authors' compilation.

center of the table at the AIIB. However, even in the AIIB, and especially with the NDB, we see examples of norms and rules that differ from the BWIs, such as South-South cooperation and alternative rules whereby the founding BRICS member-countries each make equal financial contributions and hold equal votes in the NDB, despite differences in the respective sizes of their national economies. Furthermore, the NDB, as well as China's state policy banks, allow a higher degree of policy autonomy for borrowers, unlike the Western-dominated BWIs. For example, the NDB and CDB both operate according to "host country standards," for environmental, social, and governance (ESG) safeguards. Finally, the CDB and China's central bank both support the norm of counter-cyclical financing, especially in emergency crisis scenarios, whereas the IMF has a sustained history of supporting and demanding fiscal consolidation and austerity, that is, pro-cyclical measures in both crisis and normal scenarios.

China's Growing Monetary and Financial Power

The size and reach of China's economy, its absorption of the established norms, rules, and standards of the BWIs, and its role in supporting the creation of parallel institutions have given China a unique position as a rule-taker, rule-maker, and rule-shaker in the international monetary and financial systems.

Earlier research on the role of China in the BWIs concluded that China was "playing our game," as a "rule-taker" that largely accepted the rules of the

BWIs. More recent scholarship has come to see China as a partial rule-taker and burgeoning reshaper of existing rules, or what we call a rule-shaker inside the BWIs. Some of the latest literature has examined how China is starting to work outside the BWIs to create new institutions, new rules, and norms. When it comes to the consequences for the international system or world order, the consensus in these studies is that China is still largely a status quo actor, "taking" and "reshaping" the existing rules *within* the BWIs.

We also argue that this hybrid stance – one foot in, one foot out – does grant China more voice within the BWIs and inside the existing international monetary and financial systems. However, we differ from the aforementioned studies in three respects. First, we see China's growing contributions inside the BWIs, and China's creation of new institutions and new rules outside of the BWIs, as giving China "two-way countervailing power." In conceptualizing "countervailing monetary and financial power," we draw on John Kenneth Galbraith's (1952) term "countervailing power," and the scholarship in International Political Economy that has long established that the industrialized countries hold great economic power and leverage access to their large economies to exert power over other countries (Hirschman, 1945; Strange, 1976, 1987, 1988; Cohen, 1998, 2007; Andrews, 2006; Drezner, 2007b). Galbraith's study focused on the post-war US economy, which he showed was not functioning well because of a concentration of economic power in large industrial companies. Galbraith examined how workers and input providers could form coalitions to collectively bargain and pressure the state to create regulations to introduce more market competition and make markets more efficient. Drawing on Hirschman (1970), Gallagher (2015) adapted Galbraith's concept to analyze the international monetary realm, showing how the BRICS countries exercised countervailing monetary power at the IMF to shift IMF policy on capital controls by forming new institutions outside the IMF, threatening to "exit" in terms of extra-forum leverage, and forming coalitions with key staff and other countries inside the IMF. In this Element, we expand the concept of "countervailing monetary and financial power" to examine China's behavior in both the international monetary and global development finance realms. We find that China is leveraging its domestic capabilities and international institutions in two directions simultaneously: as a rule-taker and rule-shaker *within* the BWIs, and as a rule-maker *outside* of the BWIs (see Table 2).

Second, China's hybrid positioning paves the way for China (and other countries) to exit the BW system, if or when it sees the need to. Due to China's increased capabilities within its own institutions and its own financial resources, China has increased its contributions to the World Bank, and it no longer "needs" the services of the BWIs as it did in the 1980s and 1990s. As we discuss later in this volume, China has never taken a balance of payments loan from the IMF. The combination of these factors, and the largesse and relative success that China has achieved in creating alternative institutions, has triggered the West to think that China could exit or push to rival the BWIs. Depending on how other influential members of the BWIs react to China's institutional reform efforts, inside or outside the BWIs, whether they welcome or resist them, will affect whether China and other developing countries choose to continue working within the BWIs or outside. The decision and outcomes are not preordained.

Third, we see China leveraging its influence and power to advance globally transformative changes in the direction of a less-US-centered, more diffuse, globally-diverse, negotiated, multi-centered global economic order. These trends and patterns with regard to China's taking, making, and shaking of the rules and norms are examined in more detail in the next two sections. Finally, we discuss what could happen if China continues to push ahead with its hybrid positioning. Is the West likely to continue to engage China to increase its stakeholdership in the BWIs, or treat China more as a threat? As this Element goes to press in 2025, Western governments are pushing back against China's global rise, hybrid positioning, and countervailing power, and have shifted to compete with China on the global terrain, in relations with the Global South, within the BWIs, and at the UN. We will address which outcome is more likely and what it means for China, the Global South, and the West.

2 How China Remakes the Global Monetary System

Since assuming the seat of "China" inside the IMF, the PRC has largely embraced the US dollar as the *de facto* global currency and the US dollar payments system, and has behaved as an active member in the Fund. For the last forty years, Beijing has played along as a rule-taker in the IMF, and Chinese officials have established a "professional relationship" with the Fund as a member in "good standing" by learning the rules and significantly increasing China's contributions to the IMF.[2] As an IMF member, and even while being a rule-taker, Beijing's main domestic objectives have been to pursue needed national economic reforms, maintain a sufficient degree of policy autonomy on national economic policy, and ensure economic stability inside China. However, over time, China has increasingly pushed for changes inside the IMF and for altering rules and norms in the global monetary system more broadly, which are relevant for other nations, both developing and developed.

---

[2] We thank Dong He for sharing this description of how China is perceived at the IMF: Toronto, August 2023. Chin and Gallagher cross-verified this observation with other relevant participant-observers and with related qualitative and quantitative data such as member contributions.

For forty years, China has internalized the core rules of the IMF, such as the terms of borrowing and repayment, requirements on surveillance and national economic information provision, membership contributions and quota-based voting shares, as well as adhering to some extent to the Fund's policy norms, such as on exchange rates and current and capital account opening (see Table 3). Moreover, China has largely operated in accordance with the combination of rules and norms for the dollar-centered international monetary and reserve system. But on the policies and regulations that Beijing has deemed essential for ensuring the stable management of the national economy, China has protected its policy space to determine the exact exchange rate regime, capital account regulations, monetary, macroeconomic and fiscal policies, and reserve management and foreign currency crisis-insulation strategies.

What makes China's role particularly impactful, however, is that China has also taken actions as an IMF member, acting beyond its national context to affect changes that are of direct relevance to developing country members in the IMF more broadly. Working inside the IMF, China has long advocated for increases in its voice *and* that of developing countries within the IMF. China has advocated for quota increases for itself and other developing countries as an IMF member, as well as for policy and operational changes in the Fund, such as less onerous conditionality in response to crises.

But China has also worked outside of the IMF to create new institutions, new rules, and establish alternative norms, including new lines of emergency financing outside of the IMF (see Table 3). As a new rule-maker outside of the Fund, China was a co-lead creator and member of the Chiang Mai Initiative Multilateralization (CMIM) and the BRICS Contingent Reserve Arrangement (CRA) – two new emergency liquidity funds for its member countries. Moreover, China has amassed a large, historically unprecedented foreign

Table 3 China and the Re-making of Global Monetary Affairs

	Legacy Order	**Rule-Maker**
Rule-Taker	US Dollar	CMIM/CRA linked portions
	Joining IMF	AMRO surveillance
	Technical support	Counter-Cyclical Support Facility
Rule-Shaker	SDR basket expansion	RMB Internationalization/ CIPS
	Quota Reform	CMIM/CRA governance
	Capital Account	PBOC swaps/CDB liquidity
	SDR Issuances	
	Exhange Rate Policy	

exchange reserve, which it uses for self-insurance. China has also allocated a substantial amount of these reserves to provide new liquidity through bilateral arrangements with other developing countries outside of the BWIs. The People's Bank of China (PBOC), stocked with more than US$3 trillion and other reserves, has become a liquidity supplier to other countries through a significant number of bilateral renminbi-based currency agreements and swap arrangements. More recently, the CDB has also been providing emergency liquidity and budget support for countries in debt distress across the Global South. With these new China-backed bilateral and multilateral institutional arrangements (see Table 3), which operate in parallel to the IMF and play similar functions, China has advanced new or modified rules and established alternative norms that are different from those of the IMF.

After increasing its contributions within the IMF and having created new institutions outside of the Fund, with new rules and alternative norms, China has also looked back into the IMF and leveraged its growing influence both inside and outside of the IMF to shake-up the rules or reshape the rules and the established norms within the Fund. In a growing number of instances since the late 1990s, China, as a "rule-shaker," has used such two-way leverage to lead in pushing for changes in the rules and norms within the IMF in issue-areas such as quota and voice reforms, exchange rate management, reserve management, and emergency and non-crisis liquidity provision. Working inside and outside of the IMF, China's hybrid behavior is producing outcomes that are gradually transformative in the realm and global system of international currencies. China has embraced the international use of the US dollar as a rule-taker, but it has also supported an increased role for the euro and the IMF's Special Drawing Rights (SDR) as international money and reserve currencies, calling for increased use of SDRs as emergency liquidity for developing countries in ways that have been resisted by the United States. Beijing has also advocated for an increased global role for its national currency, the renminbi (RMB), as a medium of exchange, unit of account, and store of value, including for official reserve management purposes. China has done so by pushing for the RMB's inclusion in the IMF's SDR reserve basket.

This section first details how China has acted as a rule-taker in the IMF and the existing international monetary system. It then examines how China has been a new rule-maker, creating alternative institutions that operate according to new rules and norms outside the IMF. Finally, it focuses on China as a rule-shaker back within the IMF, as the driver of fundamental modifications of existing rules and norms inside the Fund. The cumulative effect is that China and its partners have opened the door for exploring alternatives inside the IMF and exist options outside (see Table 3). The path that China will choose in the future – inside or outside the IMF – or whether it can maintain the hybrid positioning, is not preordained. Much will depend on the degree of modification that will be accepted or tolerated by the Western powers inside the IMF. But we turn first to the details of China as a rule-taker, new rule-maker, and rule-shaker in relation to the IMF.

China as Rule-Taker

China's integration into the International Monetary Fund (IMF) and its embrace of the US dollar after the late 1970s were significant changes for China *and* for the established Bretton Woods order. By entering the dollar order, the PRC was able to engage in international trade and absorb foreign direct investment to a much greater extent than during the Maoist period (1949–1976). From the 1980s onward, China built capital markets that were increasingly integrated into the global financial system. Integration into the established international monetary and reserve system combined rule-taking and norm-taking behavior for China. IMF membership enabled China to learn the rules, standards, and norms of the dollar order.

From the early 1980s to the mid-1990s, China largely behaved as a rule-taker within the IMF, adhering to the many rules and standards of the Fund. In joining the IMF, the PRC gained the benefits of Fund membership, but membership required it to also agree to obligations such as sharing data and information with the members of the Fund, subjecting itself to multilateral rules and scrutiny, and delegating a degree of its national economic sovereignty to the multilateral institution (Jacobson and Oksenberg, 1990).

In the 1980s and 1990s, China underwent rapid and dramatic national economic reforms, development, and modernization. International Relations scholars have argued that China's "socialization" to the international rules, its absorbing and internalizing of the lessons and policy norms of the IMF, and some degree of internal transformation characterized the nature of China's relations with the global institutions (Pearson 1999; Johnson, 2008). However, it is important to observe that China's "socialization" to IMF rules and norms did not occur in a static institutional context, as the IMF itself (and World Bank) were themselves undergoing profound changes from the early 1970s onward, toward "neoliberalism" and the "Washington Consensus."

The foundational academic study of China's entry and participation in the IMF (and the World Bank and the GATT) from 1945 to the decade of the 1980s, by Jacobson and Oksenberg (1990), details the PRC's original goals when it acceded to the IMF:

1. Learn the technical requirements for managing a modern, market-oriented financial system that meets international standards.

2. Gain information about other countries and their economies.
3. Reconnect with foreign economic institutions through IMF programs.
4. Expulsion of the Taipei regime from the IMF and its further marginalization in the international community.
5. Demonstrate that the PRC is a "friendly member of the international community."

The most straight-forward examples of China's internalization of IMF rules and norms pertained to the obligations of IMF membership spelled out in the "Articles of Agreement." The Articles required China to take on five dimensions of rules. First, the PRC had to ratify its membership and pay its quota to the Fund. When the PRC entered the IMF in 1980, the PRC assumed the ninth-largest quota, the largest of any developing country. Subsequently, in September 1980, the Fund authorized a special increase in the PRC's quota from SDR 550 million to SDR 1.2 billion, and then increased it further to SDR 1.8 billion in November 1980, and again to SDR 2.39 billion in 1983 (Jacobson and Oksenberg, 1990, 32, 121). As China made these membership payments and became a major shareholder of the Fund's financial resources, it took a collective interest as a prudent co-manager of the finances.

A second form of China's IMF rule-taking relates to borrowing from the Fund. China had to learn the evolving policy norms of the Fund and internalize the rules in order to minimize the effects of the IMF's policy conditionality, which is attached to the Fund's loans. The PRC absorbed the IMF's rules on the upper limit of borrowing from its allotted reserve tranche to avoid triggering a challenge from the Fund and the related need to justify the loan request based on the balance of payment needs of the borrower.[3] The IMF's conditionality is controversial because it requires the borrower to implement domestic policy changes, such as loosening exchange rates, cutting public sector employment, government subsidies, and public spending. China has avoided the IMF's conditionality. The PRC has only borrowed twice from the Fund, in the early and mid-1980s, and it has not done so since. In spring 1981, at a time when China was struggling with its post-Mao economic reforms, including balance of payments, Beijing drew from the IMF for its first credit tranche of SDR 450 million and a Trust Fund loan of SDR 309 million, for a total of SDR 759 million from the Fund's General Reserve Account (Jacobson and Oksenberg, 1990, 122).[4] In May 1983, the government

---

[3] This justification then generates a commitment from the borrower to the IMF to pursue policies which the Fund designates as the condition ("conditionality") for obtaining permission from the IMF to draw the loan.

[4] The standby arrangement was provided to support China's 1981 "Economic Stabilization Program," and the severe retrenchment measures which the Chinese government had already planned to undertake, made for efficient negotiations with the IMF Executive Board and limited

swiftly repaid the first credit tranche, and made good in full in 1984.[5] In November 1986, China borrowed SDR 600 million for purchases and a SDR 30 million loan (Ministry of Foreign Affairs of the People's Republic of China, 2000; IMF, 2021a; IMF, 2021b), repaying both in full and early.

Other IMF rule-taking that China was obligated to fulfill under the Fund's Articles included the publication of IMF materials in Chinese and their dissemination inside China to the relevant stakeholders. To meet the Article IV requirements, China had to hold bilateral discussions with the IMF, typically every year, when an IMF staff team visits the country, collects economic and financial information, and gives recommendations to the officials on the country's economic policies. China must provide a range of national economic and financial information related to its fiscal and macroeconomic situation and exchange rate policy to the IMF's Article IV team. Under Article VIII (Section v), related to the Fund's oversight of its members' exchange rate policy, China is required to collect and publish economic statistics according to the IMF's standards, and the Fund engages in exchange rate policy surveillance and provides its assessment.

Related to its annual consultations, surveillance, and advisory roles, the Fund has also provided considerable technical assistance and technical training to China in the areas of the Fund's competence. Since 1980, experts have traveled to China to conduct training sessions, and large numbers of younger Chinese officials have attended seminars and courses organized by the IMF in Washington, DC. The IMF Bureau of Statistics taught PBOC officials the concept of "balance of payments" and helped them improve their methodology for compiling balance of payments statistics according to IMF standards, as well as the central bank's related accounting practices (Jacobson and Oksenberg, 1990, 122). After "taking" the IMF procedures, PBOC officials returned to China, and compiled their balance of payments statistics using the IMF standards, though they kept the data secret (*neibu*, or internal) in 1982, 1983 and 1984. In 1985, the PBOC modified its behaviour and published the balance of payments statistics in the public domain for the first time, according to IMF norms. In due course, IMF staff continued to work closely with Chinese officials to improve their monetary supply data and external debt statistics.

---

conditions. Beijing learned that an IMF 'lending arrangement' is similar to a line of credit, and has to be approved by the IMF Executive Board, and that the borrowing member is required to observe specific terms and be subject to periodical reviews in order to continue to draw upon the arrangement; and that an 'outright loan', approved by the Board, does not require the borrower to observe specific terms.

[5] Going to back to the PRC's loans from the USSR in the 1950s, Premier Zhou Enlai made it the norm for the PRC to repay its foreign loans in full and early, and regardless of whatever economic difficulties China was facing.

Exchange rate policy is another area in which China adhered to IMF rules and norms, at least during the first-two decades. From the mid-1980s to the mid-1990s, and as advised by the IMF, China undertook rounds of adjustment for the RMB exchange rate regime. In the mid-1980s, China devalued the RMB by 15.8 percent to address its balance of payments problems during that period (Lardy, 1992). In 1996, China made the RMB freely convertible under the current account in order to comply with IMF Article VIII (PBOC 1996; IMF, 1996). China also undertook a series of policy and institutional reforms in its domestic financial sector, specifically central banking reforms and changes to corporate governance and financial legislation, as advised by the IMF, as part of the country's "economic modernization" (Lardy, 1998, 1999; Kent, 2007).

For the first-two decades, and to some extent into the next two, through the IMF borrowing schemes, technical and policy assistance dialogs, and training programs, Chinese officials absorbed and internalized the policy and technical advice, procedures and methods, governance standards, and "best practices" of the IMF (Wang, 2018). Jacobson and Oksenberg accurately described China's record of participation at the IMF (and World Bank) in the initial period of membership as an "orderly process," where both the IMF and China demonstrated a "methodical, cautious approach to building a relationship" (121, 127).

China as Rule-Maker

The 1997–98 Asian Financial Crisis (AFC) was a turning point for China's relations with the BWIs. At IMF meetings in the 1980s through the mid-1990s, China called on members to increase the use of SDR but did not take concrete action to push for expanded use of SDR. Nor did China push to alter the institutional landscape at the system level, particularly the dominant role of the IMF in the multilateral governance of global liquidity and financial safety nets. However, this changed in the aftermath of the 1997–98 Asian Financial Crisis (AFC). Working outside the IMF, China has helped to build several bilateral and multilateral arrangements that mimic the lender-of-last-resort function of the IMF, albeit with different rules and norms (Figure 1).

China's financial and central banking officials – along with their counterparts in other East Asian nations – watched how the IMF and the US responded to the AFC and drew lessons, deciding to self-insure in order to avoid having to borrow from the IMF (Chin, 2010, 2012). China and East Asian governments self-insulated by building up large stores of foreign exchange reserves, which they could draw on unilaterally without needing approval – and they could use the reserves to help others. China and Japan

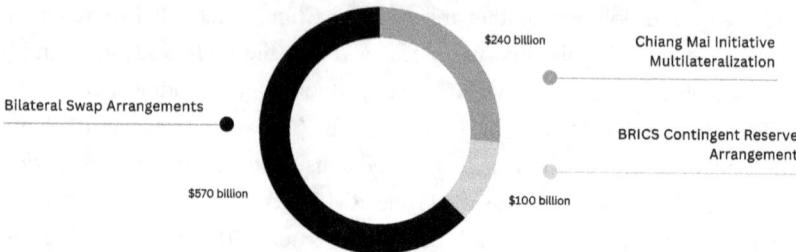

Figure 1 China's contribution to the Global Financial Safety Net (2023)
Source: Gallagher et al., 2023

have led the way among non-US nations in accumulating the largest US dollar reserves in the world.

On the multilateral front, China's approach to the global financial safety net (GFSN) shifted from focusing on appealing to the IMF for additional financing for the South to promoting the SDR as an alternative supply of global liquidity and as a reserve option. Outside the IMF, China, Japan, and the ASEAN+3 nations allocated resources and diplomatic attention to building a regional financial safety net in East Asia: the Chiang Mai Initiative (CMI), which was later further expanded with more money and more functions, and renamed as the "Chiang Mai Initiative Multilateralization" (CMIM). In October 1998, amid the ongoing AFC, China's central bank governor Dai Xianglong stood up at the joint annual discussions (IMF and World Bank) and stated China's view that the

> main cause of the crisis [AFC] is that international cooperation and the evolution of the international financial system lag far behind the economic globalization and financial integration process, and the speed of their liberalization exceeded the pace of enhancing the economic management abilities of the crisis-hit countries ... Speculators with huge sums of capital are able to take large leveraged positions to control and manipulate markets for profit, accentuating market volatility ... the international community has [still] not come to a consensus on effective mechanisms for the monitoring and containment of risks brought about by volatile capital flows.

Dai then offered: "It is our firm belief that by strengthening coordination and mutual support within the Asian region, the economic and financial development in Asia is bound to stabilize gradually" (IMF, 1998).

The agreement to create the CMI was announced in May 2000 at the ASEAN+3 finance ministers' meeting. China, together with Japan, was the co-initiator of the CMI. In December 1998, at the second informal meeting of ASEAN+3 in Vietnam, China's then Vice President Hu Jintao proposed that ASEAN+3 finance and central bank deputies meet to discuss further regional cooperation, and they did so in April 1999. In November 1999, at the third informal meeting of ASEAN+3 Leaders in Manila, China's Premier Zhu Rongji suggested that the bloc should discuss how to institutionalize their regional economic and financial cooperation. In December 1999, the finance ministers agreed to establish "self-help and support mechanisms in East Asia."

The CMI originally consisted of 15 bilateral swap agreements, totaling the equivalent of US$37.5 billion, including a US$1 billion ASEAN Swap. "Equivalent" because, although the majority of the CMI financing was in US dollars, Beijing struck a unique agreement with the CMI partners that the bilateral swap lines with China and other CMI partners be denominated in RMB. Despite the fact that East Asian countries have independently funded and managed the CMI, the expanded CMIM can still be conceptualized as having links to the IMF, in that the ASEAN+3 grouping decided to tie a portion of any future disbursement of the Chiang Mai funds to IMF approval (initially set at 90 percent of the borrowing quota requiring IMF approval and subject to IMF conditionality).

However, the intention of ASEAN+3 from the outset of the CMI discussions was to increase the operational autonomy of the CMI, away from the IMF, over time. In the two decades since CMI's creation, ASEAN+3 has gradually increased the portion of CMI(M) swaps that can be allocated without IMF approval (Grimes and Kring, 2020). In May 2005, ASEAN+3 agreed to integrate economic surveillance procedures into the CMI framework and, importantly for increasing operational autonomy beyond the IMF, agreed to create an ASEAN+3 economic monitoring and advisory office called the "ASEAN+3 Macroeconomic Research Office" (AMRO). Relatedly, ASEAN+3 agreed to increase the size of swaps that could be withdrawn without an IMF-supported program from the original 10 percent to 20 percent (ASEAN+3, 2005). ASEAN+3 finance ministers further agreed to significantly increase the size of the swaps in the CMI, and by 2007, the size of the CMI swap pool had doubled to US$64 billion and 16 swap agreements.

After the 2008–09 GFC, China and the ASEAN+3 further boosted the CMI into CMIM, increasing the size of the regional swap fund from US$90 billion to US$120 billion. Importantly, the grouping moved ahead on "multilateralizing" the bilateral swap agreements into a "single [regionalized pool] contractual agreement." CMIM took effect in March 2010 (AMRO, 2023). CMIM's core objectives are (1) to address balance of payment and/or short-term liquidity difficulties in the ASEAN+3 region; and (2) to supplement existing international financial arrangements. China's contribution (including Hong Kong) to the CMIM increased to US$38.4 billion. For some comparative perspective, the size of the CMIM at US$120 billion was relatively small compared to the national reserves of the Asian countries (US$5 trillion) and paled in comparison to the amounts deployed by G20 national governments and the ECB in response to the GFC – China's domestic stimulus package alone was the equivalent of US$586 billion. Nonetheless, the increase in the size of the East Asian regional safety net required striking a new diplomatic consensus between China and Japan, as the two largest "co-contributors," Korea (US$19.2 billion), and the ASEAN nations with a combined US$24 billion (Chin, 2012).

The ASEAN+3 opened the ASEAN+3 Macroeconomic Research Office (AMRO) as a regional office for the CMIM in April 2011 in Singapore. The creation of this office was especially significant, as it signaled the ability to delegate surveillance and loan design, that is, new rule-making, to a self-governed body – a prerequisite for ending the CMIM's subordination to the IMF (Grimes and Kring, 2020). To kick-start the rule-making, the ASEAN+3 finance ministers decided on the new basic rules for activating the swap agreements and the new rules for joint decision-making on their use (as a "first step toward multilateralization"), and delegated it to AMRO to work on the details and bring the proposals back to the ASEAN+3 finance ministers for decision-making.

One of the most noteworthy new rules of the CMIM relates to the activation and delivery of CMIM swaps, which makes the first draw on the CMIM immediate, rapid, targeted, and easy to access for the borrower, with more extensive justification required for a second draw. The technical reason for this approach is that crisis financing must be provided rapidly to help avert or contain a financial crisis. However, AMRO staff also gave "Asian"-specific cultural reasons for how the ASEAN+3 members of CMIM approach the broader issue of the stigma that becomes attached to the borrower that draws on emergency crisis liquidity in an actual crisis scenario: that rapid and easy access to crisis liquidity, and fast delivery of the first draw, can help to reduce the reputational stigma that is attached to borrowers of IMF-type loans and allow for national "face-saving," which is said to be especially important in East Asian cultures.[6] As no ASEAN+3 member has drawn on the CMIM to date, there is yet to be a concrete case study of the delivery of this emergency fund. Nonetheless, the intention to devise rules that are informed by IMF rules and norms, but are more responsive to "Asian cultural characteristics," can be observed.

In 2014, the ASEAN Plus Three decided to further increase the size of the CMIM by doubling it to $240 billion and also to increase the CMIM-IMF De-Linked Portion to 30 percent, as well as to extend the maturity and supporting

---

[6] The author's interviews with AMRO staff: AMRO, Singapore, July 2012.

period (AMRO, 2023) The ASEAN+3 also expanded the purpose of the regional safety net by introducing the "CMIM Precautionary Line," a new *crisis prevention* facility, adding to the existing "CMIM Stability Facility," aimed at *crisis resolution*. In March 2021, members also amended the CMIM Agreement to increase the IMF De-Linked Portion from 30 percent to 40 percent. Importantly, they also agreed to use their own local currencies for CMIM financing, in addition to the US dollar (see Figure 1). China and the other ASEAN+3 members have further indicated that they intend to completely de-link the disbursement of CMIM funds from IMF approval (Grimes and Kring, 2020). The ASEAN+3 members are now discussing how to further expand their financial cooperation under the CMIM umbrella, which would mean new purposes, more new rules, and norms.

The CMIM has, in turn, inspired the BRICS nations to create their own US$100 billion Contingent Reserve Arrangement (CRA) as a similar emergency liquidity pool for the BRICS governments (see Figure 1). The former Brazilian Executive Director at the IMF and former Vice President of the NDB, Paulo Nogueira Batista Jr., writes that the CMI was *the* model that BRICS governments drew on to create their own liquidity safety net (Batista Jr., 2021, 13–32). Batista Jr. visited the AMRO in Singapore in 2014 to learn about the CMIM first-hand, where he, Brazilian finance officials, and China's central bank and finance officials relayed the lessons to the BRICS group.

The CRA was officially launched in 2015, with China, by far the largest committed contributor, allocating US$41 billion, while Brazil, India, and Russia agreed to each commit US$18 billion, and South Africa US$5 billion.[7] The BRICS governments set the amount that each country can draw from the CRA fund and the associated voting share for each member. Of particular note, China made a financial contribution that far outweighs its agreed access amount: after giving US$41 billion, China agreed to only draw up to US$21 billion if needed. This rule is underpinned by a new norm of international leadership that China is advancing of "giving more, taking less"; the PRC's take on global leadership as sacrificing for the greater good and being generous in providing global public goods (Chin and Stubbs, 2011). With its sizable national foreign reserves, Beijing does not need the CRA for insurance. The BRICS Plus members are now discussing adding more member-states to the CRA and expanding the size of the fund, and some researchers are discussing expanding the financial uses for the CRA beyond emergency crisis liquidity to non-crisis use, which means creating new rules and new norms among the CRA members.

---

[7] "Commited" because the funds for the CRA are callable, not already delivered to a central deposit.

In the *informal* realm of global governance, China has also played a role in creating alternative rules and norms to the IMF in response to the 2008–09 Great Financial Crisis. China acted as a new rule-maker, outside of the IMF, when it pushed for a portion of the US$1.1 trillion agreed upon by G20 country leaders for emergency economic fire-fighting to be allocated to regional institutions to deliver, rather than to the IMF (Chin, 2010, 2012). When the GFC erupted, leaders of the BRICS nations, especially Indian PM Singh and Brazilian President Lula emphasized that the GFC was not caused by developing countries, and that developing countries should not have to pay the price. Indonesia, China, India, South Korea, and Brazil pushed G20 leaders to support the creation of new lines of rapid, flexible counter-cyclical lines of emergency financing for developing and low-income countries but to be dispersed by regional development banks, not the IMF (Chin, 2012).

China supported an Indonesian proposal to the G20 to allocate a portion of the new money promised to the IMF (at the April 2009 London G20 Summit) to the Asian Development Bank (ADB) instead. This financing would be *flexible, fast-disbursing, and utilize front-loaded instruments* that provide *rapid assistance* to developing countries in the Asian region that were considered "well-governed," but nonetheless faced potential balance of payments crises due to the GFC.[8] With the backing of the G20, the ADB quickly created a new countercyclical instrument – the Countercyclical Support Facility – to provide budget support of up to US$3 billion for crisis-affected countries in Asia (ADB, 2009). However, the new "rule" for Asia had a broader global impact, as regional development banks in other regions of the world, such as the IDB and the AfDB, quickly followed the ADB's example. They also drew on a portion of the new funds committed at the London G20 and established new regional-level facilities to provide rapid and more flexible counter-cyclical lines of credit to countries in their regions. These regional mechanisms prevented further contagion and helped to contain spillovers across the regions.

China has also initiated other new elements of the global financial safety net at the bilateral level (see Figure 1). When several of China's trading partners experienced a liquidity crunch and a crisis of trade finance in 2008 and 2009 because of the global liquidity freeze, a number of these governments turned to Beijing for help, and to the PBOC specifically for emergency liquidity support. Like the US Federal Reserve, which offered emergency US dollar swap lines to US trading partners in periods of economic and financial uncertainty, the PBOC agreed to several bilateral currency agreements, denominated in RMB, including bilateral swap agreements (BSAs). However, the PBOC currency agreements are

---

[8] Author's discussions with Chatib Basri, March 2010.

different from the US dollar swaps of the US Federal Reserve in that the RMB can be used for a wider range of purposes, such as "non-emergency" trade financing.

RMB-denominated BSAs were first signed with South Korea in 2008, and then with Argentina, Belarus, Hong Kong, Indonesia, and Malaysia in 2009. These countries were all confronting looming balance of payments crises amid the GFC, and the BSAs helped them avoid a full-on crisis. For these countries, settling their cross-border payments with business partners in China using RMB or their own national currency meant that an equivalent number of US dollars was freed-up to be used elsewhere.[9] In 2011, the PBOC signed more BSAs with other countries that were also facing balance of payments challenges due to the residual effects of the GFC, including Kazakhstan, Mongolia, Pakistan, and Thailand.[10] In 2010, the PBOC signed a BSA with Singapore to support the city-state's desire to join Hong Kong as an offshore RMB transaction hub. Britain signed a bilateral currency swap agreement with the PBOC in June 2013 for similar reasons. In October 2013, the ECB also signed a bilateral RMB-Euro currency swap agreement as a liquidity backstop.

Starting in 2013, some of these governments drew on their PBOC swap lines, beginning with Pakistan, which reportedly used the RMB equivalent of US$600 million from its RMB 10 billion (US$1.5 billion) swap line with the PBOC and exchanged the RMB for US dollars. Facing a sharp decrease in its foreign exchange reserves, the State Bank of Pakistan did so to shore up its reserves, boost market confidence in the Pakistani economy, and gain approval for a US$6.65 billion IMF loan in June 2013 (Rana, 2013). In 2015, Argentina was the next government to use its PBOC BSA for external liquidity when it was blocked from capital markets after defaulting on its sovereign debt. The PBOC allowed the Central Bank of Argentina (BCRA) to draw the RMB equivalent of US$2.7 billion from its RMB 70 billion (US$11 billion) swap line. Argentina used some of the RMB to pay for imports from China, which allowed the BCRA to keep its dollar reserves for other purposes and exchange some of the RMB into US dollars (Reuters, 2014; Devereaux, 2015). Also in 2015, when Mongolia's raw material exports waned, foreign investment fell, and foreign exchange reserves ran low, Mongolia drew the RMB equivalent of US$1.7 billion from its US$2.5 billion swap line with China. A senior

---

[9] The 2009 PBOC-HKMA swap renewal was the exception as Hong Kong actually ran-out of RMB in 2009 due to the Mainland's capital controls, and it needed access to more RMB offshore to backstop the growing offshore RMB payments transactions.

[10] New Zealand was the exception in 2011, as it was not facing balance of payment challenges, rather New Zealand authorities wanted the BSA as a RMB liquidity backstop for New Zealand business to participate in international use of RMB.

economist at the Central Bank of Mongolia noted that the BSA was "one of the tools to absorb the shock of the balance of payments pressures" (Edwards, 2015).

Russia's central bank accessed its BSA with the PBOC on various occasions from October 2015 to March 2016, after Western sanctions and falling oil prices put downward pressure on the ruble from 2014 onward (Xinhua, 2016). The amount of Russian drawings was not reported publicly, and China's *Xinhua News Agency* only noted that the money was allocated to several Russian and Chinese counterparties to support bilateral trade and direct investment between the two nations (CBR, 2016). Ukraine also drew on its BSA with China in 2016, when Kyiv's foreign exchange reserves fell below the IMF-mandated reserve target, and it gained approval from the PBOC to activate the swap with China (IMF, 2016, 7; McDowell, 2019, 136).

These examples show when, where, how, and why China's swap agreements have served as lender-of-last-resort mechanisms outside the IMF for five countries that chose to activate a portion of their RMB swap lines for short-term needs: Argentina, Mongolia, Pakistan, Russia, and Ukraine. The Ukraine case was an example of linking a PBOC BSA to maintaining an IMF loan. There are other cases where a BSA from China was key for the partner country to secure an IMF loan, namely Pakistan and Mongolia. In November 2016, China also signed a BSA with Egypt, which opened the door for Cairo to secure an IMF credit line of US$12 billion. The IMF required Egypt to secure US$6 billion in bilateral liquidity before approving Egypt's IMF program (IMF 2017; Reuters, 2016).

These swap lines continued through the COVID-19 pandemic period and the subsequent shocks, and an increasing number of countries also drew on those lines. China's swaps and its other new lines of financing, particularly from China's state policy banks, such as the China Development Bank, have become important sources of crisis-related liquidity as an alternative to the IMF (Sundquist, 2021). Kaplan (2021) finds that China's liquidity loans have given Latin American countries more room to maneuver recover, and avoid borrowing from the IMF. In 2008, after Ecuador was shut out of private capital markets, China provided a liquidity loan to help Ecuador return to the private capital markets more quickly than if it had undergone austerity measures from the IMF (Gallagher, 2016). By the end of 2023, the PBOC had over $400 billion in active currency swaps, with several developing countries benefiting from this liquidity finance, including Pakistan, Egypt, and Indonesia. Interestingly, in 2023, a swap agreement with the PBOC allowed Argentina to draw $2.7 billion to bridge its IMF program (Zucker Marques and Kring, 2023). In 2024, Egypt also benefited from crisis-related financing from China, which helped secure Egypt's US$8 billion IMF loan.

Working outside the IMF, China and its partners are advancing new rules and policy norms that serve as an *alternative* to the IMF, whether it is in the small- and medium-sized developing countries using bilateral currency agreements for emergency liquidity or trade financing, or with the CMIM and the BRICS CRA. China is acting as a new rule-maker and, in some cases, offering its own national currency, the RMB, rather than US dollars, along with the new rules. The country has also been adding new tiers and institutions to the GFSN, which creates the potential for China and partner countries to work outside of the IMF and the dollar, and according to a new set of rules and norms for lender-of-last-resort or nonemergency financing.

China as Rule-Shaker

China's efforts at building alternative institutional arrangements, rules, and norms outside of the IMF have fed-back into the IMF. In some instances, the transmission back inside was intentional on the part of China's officials. In other cases, it was not consciously undertaken by Chinese officials and their Southern partners but occurred rather through the force of example or was transmitted back by IMF staff, other officials, or national delegates inside the BWIs. The key outcome of this rule-shaking pattern is that the feed-back of the alternative rules, norms, and models actually results in changes to the rules and norms back inside the IMF. These changes represent an incremental altering – a shaking – of the established rules, norms, the preferred models, and lessons inside the Fund, in ways that reflect the rule and normative preferences of China and its Southern partners, or the experiences of the China-supported alternative institutions.

Four cases of "rule-shaking" provide examples of this pattern of behavior and outcome: first, quota and share reform in IMF governance (see Table 4); second, exchange rate policy; third, capital account policy; fourth, reserve management, including expanding the role of the SDR and the international use of China's renminbi. These changes in the rules were actually preceded by normative shifts in the IMF, such as in the balance of power norms within the IMF decision-making structures and governance processes, that have given greater voice to "the Rest" and reduced US dominance.

Quota and Voice Reform

China's rule-shaking in the IMF started after the 1997–98 Asian Financial Crisis (AFC), when it called once again for giving more voice to developing countries at a time when China and many Asian governments and citizens criticized the

Table 4 China's quota shares at IMF

	2007		2021
United States	17.1	United States	17.4
Japan	6.1	Japan	6.5
Germany	6.0	**China**	**6.4**
France	4.9	Germany	5.6
United Kingdom	4.9	France	4.2
China	**3.7**	United Kingdom	4.2

Fund's response to the AFC. This required changing the norms of the global balance of representation inside the IMF (and World Bank) away from Western dominance. In October 1999, at the Joint Annual Discussion of the IMF and World Bank, PBOC Governor Dai stated that the "operations of the international monetary system and its reform should not be controlled by a few member countries," and the "voice of the developing countries should not be neglected" (IMF, 1999). The PBOC Governor emphasized that developing countries "should be more involved in the process ... if the developed countries ... solely call on these countries for opening markets, the developing countries may encounter new crises." Dai added that developing countries "should not be forced to restructure their economies according to the developed countries' standards."

A decade later, China's leader, along with Brazilian President Luiz Inácio Lula da Silva, Indian Prime Minister Manmohan Singh, and Russian President Dmitri Medvedev, advocated for IMF governance reform at the first G20 Leaders Summit in October 2008. At successive G20 Summits, President Hu Jintao and the senior Chinese leadership coordinated with the other BRICS leaders to push for IMF and World Bank quota reforms. Working inside the Fund itself, China's representatives coordinated informally with BRICS partners to press for the rebalancing. The Brazilian Executive Director at the IMF, Paulo Nogueira Batista Jr., and the Indian Executive Director, Rakesh Mohan, took the lead in pushing for governance rebalancing inside the Fund, and China's ED supported the BRICS partners to push for changes in representation (Batista Jr., 2021). China's economic heft gave critical mass and gravitas to the vocal calls from the Brazilian and Indian EDs. In 2011, Central Bank Governor Zhou Xiaochuan called on "all parties, in the spirit of cooperation," to "fulfill the [October 2009] Pittsburgh [G20] Summit's commitment of the shift in quotas and the protection of the poorest countries' voices," and complete the

14th General Review of Quotas before the November 2010 G20 Summit. Zhou underlined, "only with the completion of the quota reform would broader governance reform be based on a solid foundation, and the overall legitimacy, accountability, and effectiveness of the IMF be credibly secured" (Zhou, 2010). In December 2015, nearly five years later, and after the NDB and CRA were launched, US lawmakers authorized the IMF 2010 quota and governance reforms, and the legislation came into effect on 1 October 2016. US lawmakers acknowledged that the US Congress only agreed to the IMF quota reforms – that is, a shake-up of IMF voice – after they saw that "China and others" had gone ahead to create their own international financial institutions (Gallagher, 2015).

Exchange Rate Policy

China has also initiated a shake-up of exchange rate rules and norms at the IMF. In 2006 and 2007, China was able to stave off the IMF's plan that would have called on China to revalue its purportedly "misaligned" exchange rate (RMB/US dollar) (Blustein, 2012). China criticized the Fund's formula for calculating the value of exchange rates, determining alignment/misalignment, and identifying manipulation, and countered that the Fund did not sufficiently take account of local factors and conditions when assessing exchange rates. Additionally, China argued that the Fund's formula relied too much on an uncertain forecast about the future current account. Furthermore, China defended the right of IMF members to pick their own exchange rate regime and rebutted the Fund's preference for free-floating exchange rates. China called instead for exchange rate stability and predictability, advocating for managed floating and bound bands within which exchange rates should move. Chinese officials further retorted that the "problem of global imbalances was caused in large part by the United States and should be dealt with primarily by the United States taking appropriate policy actions" (IMF, 2006, 19–20). From Beijing's view, the IMF was not acting as a "neutral, even-handed, fair arbiter" of international policy surveillance and coordination, but as an instrument of US foreign economic policy.[11]

The US and the G7 governments pressured the IMF Executive Board to approve the "2007 Decision on Bilateral Surveillance," over the objections of China (and Iran and Egypt) (Bluestein, 2012; Wang, 2018). China's officials, in turn, rejected the IMF 2007 "Decision" and withdrew from the bilateral surveillance exercise in 2007 and 2008 (IMF, 2007; Foot and Walter, 2011). Chinese officials stated that the PBOC had already undertaken moderate adjustments of the RMB/dollar exchange rate from 2006 onward, and they retorted that the

---

[11] Interview with former IMF Independent Evaluation Office Director Thomas Bernes, July 2009.

RMB exchange rate was at equilibrium (accurately reflecting supply and demand). China further countered, saying that IMF surveillance should be redirected to the macroeconomic and financial sector policies of the reserve currency-issuing nations (READ: the United States) and the regulations and policies of the major financial centers.

However, the IMF's pressure on China for appreciation ceased in mid-2008, with the onset of the GFC. Blustein (2012) writes that the diplomatic impasse was "conveniently resolved" when the 2008–09 GFC took a strangle-hold of the US and UK financial systems, and US Treasury Secretary Henry Paulson turned to China for help in responding to the GFC. The recently appointed IMF MD Dominique Strauss-Kahn also looked to Beijing as the GFC intensified in 2008, and Strauss-Kahn and US officials toned-down their statements on the RMB exchange rate. In 2008, the IMF dropped the "2007 Decision on Bilateral Surveillance." Some commentators, such as Blustein (2013), saw the outcome as a "lost cause," but the deeper significance was that China had successfully repelled the IMF (and US Treasury) pressure, shaking the enforcement of the Fund's rules, norms, and standards, and reshaping them toward China's preferences. In the period since the GFC, China has continued to gradually reform its exchange rate regime in the direction of a less managed float, but it has also continued to advocate for a more secure, stable, and predictable global exchange rate regime. Neither the IMF nor the US has been able to force China to adopt a fully-flexible exchange rate regime. Developing countries in Asia, Latin America, and Africa have noticed China's resolve and success in shaking and reshaping the IMF's exchange rate management and its advocacy for "managed flexibility."

Capital Account Policy

China and the other BRICS countries have advocated for a shift away from the IMF's normative preference for completely free and open capital accounts, as well as the IMF's loan rules and policy conditionality in responding to financial crises, which demand that borrowing governments undertake foreign financial and investment deregulatory measures and pro-cyclical fiscal policies – that is, reduced public spending and increased taxation (and increased spending and reduced taxes during expansionary periods). China has instead advocated for partially managed capital flows as the policy and regulatory norm, and for governments to enact counter-cyclical fiscal and monetary policy measures to counteract the economic cycle when the economy is slowing down or in crisis – namely, increasing government spending and cutting taxes to help stimulate economic recovery. Relatedly, China argues that the IMF should provide counter-cyclical emergency financial support during crises. China is willing to accept more open capital flows, largely flowing freely in and out of national economies during normal circumstances, but believes that some controls should be allowed and reapplied in crisis scenarios to help prevent or contain destabilizing hot money inflows or outflows.

In 1997, the major shareholders of the IMF almost triggered an amendment to the Articles of Agreement that would have eliminated the ability of countries to regulate capital flows. However, the role that capital account openness played in the Asian Financial Crisis and major pushback from developing countries stopped that effort. After the 2008–09 GFC, the BRICS and other Asian and Southern coalitions called for a review of the IMF's stance on capital account liberalization and capital controls. Because of their efforts in building alternative emergency liquidity arrangements outside of the IMF, as discussed in the preceding section, these coalitions could then exercise countervailing influence back inside the IMF. They succeeded in shaking up the rules within the Fund on capital controls and appropriate policy responses to contain financial crises, and in forcing the IMF to partially change its stance on lending practices and its associated policy lessons and conditionalities.

In line with China's shake-up of the rules on capital controls, the IMF Board deemed that capital account liberalization was not appropriate in all country circumstances and that the use of capital controls – rebranded as "capital flow management measures" – was said to be appropriate in some limited circumstances (Gallagher, 2015). Gallagher (2015) showed that these incremental changes were the result of direct pressure and countervailing influence, with the BRICS exerting extra-forum leverage through the simultaneous creation of the NDB and CRA, as well as their maneuvering at the G20 and back into the IMF. Inside the IMF, Fund staff aligned with the BRICS, where their research showed that capital account liberalization was associated with financial instability in developing countries, and conversely, the countries that deployed capital controls during the GFC were among the less affected (see also Grabel, 2018).

But there was a second related shift in the IMF's norms and rules on the appropriate response to financial crises that was also caused by China's shake-up of the rules. In April 2018, in a speech at the University of Hong Kong, IMF Managing Director Lagarde offered the shift from the IMF's pre-2008–09 GFC economic orthodoxy. Lagarde mentioned the improved conditions for global growth but also emphasized, "we must use the current window of opportunity to prepare for the challenges ahead," highlighting the need to build counter-cyclical monetary and fiscal **"policy buffers,"** and "creating more room to act when the next downturn inevitably comes" (IMF, 2018, bold in original). The IMF chief noted that recent studies had shown such fiscal and monetary buffers can substantially limit the loss of output in future economic crises and recessions, and that "global buffers" are needed. Rather than adhering to the IMF's traditional reputation for harsh loan conditionality – demanding spending cuts, fiscal retrenchment, budget deficit reductions, and the opening of capital markets and domestic sectors as the standard response to financial crises and economic difficulties – the IMF had come around to recognize the instabilities and shortcomings of financial markets. It agreed to support the operationalizing of stronger capital controls in severe crisis scenarios and accepted countercyclical financial interventions, increased social transfers, and income tax relief as part of its redefinition of "appropriate" fiscal and monetary policy (Clift, 2018).

In 2023, the IMF issued two documents that reinforced the IMF's normative shift on capital controls and countercyclicality, as China had consistently demanded for more than two decades. In March 2023, the IMF published the staff Working Paper titled "Capital Controls in Times of Crisis – Do They Work?" coauthored by Bhargava, Bouis, Kokenyne, Perez-Archila, Rawat, and Sahay. The paper answered "yes." It starts with the statement that "large and sudden capital outflows can pose significant economic and policy challenges to emerging markets and developing economies"; that "facing an imminent crisis, temporary capital controls on outflows may help prevent a free fall of the exchange rate, preserve foreign exchange reserves and liquidity in the financial system, and provide breathing space while needed macro-financial policies are implemented." Their related key finding and recommendation is that "countries with pervasive controls before the start of the crisis are shielded compared to countries with more open capital accounts, which see a significant decline in capital flows during crises." In April 2023, the IMF issued the staff Working Paper "Revisiting the Countercyclicality of Fiscal Policy," which detailed differing countercyclical measures as "the appropriate fiscal response" to "adverse events," as can be seen by the experience gained during recent "severe crises" (Jalles et al., 2023). The IMF Staff authors acknowledged that before the GFC, "discretionary fiscal responses were deemed too slow or hard to unwind, and automatic stabilizers were considered sufficient." But coming around to China's stance on policy norms and associated rules, the IMF staff write that, "during the unprecedented global shock of the [COVID-19] pandemic, political consensus made it possible to deploy even more rapid, diverse and novel measures." Moreover, "fiscal interventions during the [GFC] shored up private sector balance sheets and stimulated aggregate demand at a time when monetary policy in advanced economies was constrained. These suggest that fiscal policy can be swift and forceful during crises, pointing to a possible greater stabilization role of fiscal policy than in typical recessions." The paper sums up, "the experience during the recent severe crises have therefore led to a re-assessment of fiscal responses."

Reserve Management

Less widely understood is how China acts as a rule-shaker and re-shaper of the international monetary system, and potentially the dollar order, by advancing incremental changes within the IMF's reserve management norms that have the potential to incrementally transform the global monetary order over the medium-term. China has campaigned on behalf of transitioning to a more diverse and diffused global monetary and reserve system – i.e., less centralized and less unitary than the dollar order – with increased roles for the euro, the SDR, and the RMB. Its preferred outcome would be to see the dollar lose some of its lead as the leading global currency and transition to a more multi-currency system. Such a scenario would pressure the United States to behave differently in managing its domestic economy and address its massive debt load and fiscal situation. However, it would still be a global monetary order that primarily works through the institutional arrangements of the IMF and its international currency and reserve management arrangements.

Beijing has long advocated for the SDR to play an expanded role, especially for providing added emergency liquidity from the IMF to debt-wracked developing countries, going back to the 1990s. Each decade, China has advocated for new issuances of SDRs. China's representatives to the IMF made brief statements about the SDR in the 1980s and 1990s but returned to calling for expanding the use of the SDR in the aftermath of the 1997–98 AFC. From October 1999 to October 2008, China's representatives repeatedly stood at the IMFC and called for increased allocations of SDR and expanded use of SDR. At the October 1999 Joint Annual Discussion of the IMF and World Bank, PBOC Governor Dai outlined China's view of the inherent instability in the IMS due to the reliance on the US dollar as the *de facto* global currency, stating: "The role of the international reserve currency played by a few countries' national currency [READ: US dollar] has been a major source of instability in the international monetary system" (IMF, 1999). These calls by PBOC Governors, senior Finance Ministry officials, and China's IMF Executive Directors gained little notice among the Northern powers before the GFC.

Going into the London G20 Summit (2) in March 2009, China's central bank issued a statement from Governor Zhou Xiaochuan calling for reform of the international monetary and reserve system and named the SDR as a preferred option. Released amid the GFC, this statement caught global attention. Brazil and India also advocated for increasing the pool of SDR under the IMF to add emergency liquidity to the system in response to the GFC. At the London G20 Summit in April 2009, G20 Leaders "agreed to treble the resources available to the IMF to US$750 billion, to support a new SDR allocation of US$250 billion" (G20 Joint Communique, April 2009: 1). G20 Leaders also agreed "to support a general SDR allocation which will inject $250 billion into the world economy and increase global liquidity ..." (G20 Joint Communique, April 2009: 5). In July 2009, the IMF Executive Board "backed the general allocation of SDRs equivalent to US$250 billion to provide liquidity to the global economic system by supplementing Fund's member countries' foreign exchange reserves," "following the commitment made by G20 Leaders ... to boost global liquidity and welcomed by the IMFC." In August 2009, the Board of Governors of the IMF approved the general allocation (IMF, 2009). Of the SDR equivalent to US$250 billion, nearly US$100 billion of the general allocation was allocated to "emerging markets and developing countries, of which low-income countries [received] over US$18 billion."

Alongside China's rule-shaking advocacy for the SDR, Beijing also lobbied for the RMB's inclusion in the SDR basket. China's first attempt to push for the inclusion of a currency in the SDR was not successful. In November 2010, the IMF Executive Board completed the quinquennial review of the SDR valuation, and Executive Directors concluded that "although China has become the third largest exporter of goods and services on a five-year average basis and has taken steps to facilitate international use of the currency [RMB], the Chinese renminbi does not currently meet the criteria to be a freely usable currency, and it would therefore not be included in the SDR basket at this time." After this failed attempt, PBOC officials enacted a number of reforms to make the RMB more "freely usable" in international trade and direct investment transactions, as well as for trading in foreign exchange and capital markets, both offshore and onshore. These currency reforms from 2011 to 2018 have loosened controls over the cross-border and offshore flow of RMB, the convertibility of the RMB, and the RMB exchange rate, all to make the RMB more usable globally.

China also coordinated with BRICS allies around the 2011 BRICS Leaders Summit in Sanya, Hainan Province, China, to issue the group's boldest call for international monetary and reserve reforms, including expanding the SDR basket. Most importantly, 2011–2015 saw tangible increases in the international use of the RMB for cross-border trade settlement, trade finance, foreign direct investment, and treasury management, with the RMB surpassing the Japanese yen as the fourth most used currency for global payments. Beijing then leveraged the increasing use of the RMB in the global economy and the BRICS collective pressure outside of the IMF, in combination with a diplomatic push inside IMF circles. China secured key diplomatic support from key Western

European G7 states for the RMB's inclusion in the SDR basket, namely Germany, Britain, France, and Italy.

Beijing supported Christine Lagarde's nomination for IMF Managing Director, and in July 2011, Lagarde, the former French finance minister, became the eleventh Managing Director of the IMF and the first woman to hold the post. China gained a key ally at the top of the IMF in pushing for RMB/SDR inclusion and broader IMS reform. In 2012, the IMF staff in the Monetary and Capital Markets Department (2012, 12) pressed China for more changes. But as Lagarde's term as IMF Managing Director unfolded, the IMF Policy Department and its Monetary and Capital Markets Department were pressed into direct negotiations with the PBOC. The PBOC pressed the Fund to rethink the criteria and formula for inclusion, specifically on how to define "freely usable" currency. China and the IMF gradually built new consensus on the terms and conditions for the RMB to be admitted into the SDR basket. In brief, the IMF changed the rules for inclusion in the SDR basket to provide the technical rationale for the RMB's admission.

In 2012–2013, Beijing helped to bail out the eurozone, which was mired in numerous sovereign debt crises (Helleiner, 2015; Chin, 2017). The diplomatic *quid pro quo* was that the leading nations of the eurozone agreed to help China with the internationalization of the RMB and the inclusion of the RMB in the SDR. UK Chancellor of the Exchequer George Osborne made sure the City of London was not left standing outside. The European G7 members eventually brought Japan onside to support RMB/SDR inclusion in 2014, essentially leaving the US isolated diplomatically. By 2015, the US Treasury relented and agreed it would no longer block the RMB's addition to the SDR basket.

With the RMB's inclusion in the SDR basket, China is in a stronger position to advocate for further rule changes to expand the role of the SDR within the operations of the IMF and in the global monetary and reserve system. To the extent that China succeeds in this effort of turning the SDR, which is still largely a reserve accounting tool, into a multilateral reserve asset option, China is helping to further multilateralize the global monetary system and promote de facto de-dollarization over the medium term.

Finally, when considering the venues and channels of China's rule-shaking inside the IMF, one should also consider the *joint* technical assistance and capacity-building initiatives that China's central bank and finance ministry have established with the IMF. This includes the new Beijing-based China-IMF Capacity Development Center (CICDC), opened in 2018 and dedicated to providing technical assistance and training tailored to support the China-led BRI. The training curriculum and schedule at the CICDC are jointly decided by Fund staff and PBOC officials in a manner that can be called "two-way mutual socialization." IMF Managing Director Lagarde stated in May 2017 at the first Belt and Road Forum (BRF) in Beijing that the BRI "aims to connect economies, communities, and people. It holds great potential to bring benefits in terms of high-quality infrastructure, inclusiveness, and economic cooperation" (IMF, 2017). The IMF head said that the new IMF-China Center would support the BRI by "providing policy advice, financial support as appropriate, and hands-on training and capacity building – so that economies can maximize the benefits of more investment, trade, and financial connectivity, while maintaining economic and financial stability." According to Lagarde, the PBOC and the IMF established the CICDC to "support effective institution-building and policy-making in countries along the Belt and Road and beyond." By April 2019, the CICDC had already trained more than 140 officials from 45 countries.

China's internalization of IMF (and World Bank) "sustainability" norms was evidenced in the "Debt Sustainability Framework for Participating Countries of the Belt and Road Initiative," which was issued by China's Ministry of Finance in March 2019 for assessing future BRI project proposals and drew almost entirely from the IMF-World Bank debt sustainability frameworks.[12] At the same time, Beijing had prevailed in getting the IMF Managing Director to commit, at the second BRF in April 2019, to China's agenda, when Lagarde announced that the IMF would help with "the next phase" of the BRI, specifically by "training on debt management and green sustainability related to BRI infrastructure and other projects" (IMF, 2019). Lagarde suggested that the IMF could help improve the "BRI 2.0" with "stronger frameworks" ranging from "increased transparency, open procurement with competitive bidding, and better risk assessment in project selection."

3 How China Remakes Global Development Finance

China was "present at the creation" of the Bretton Woods Institutions in 1944, represented by Kuomintang officials and Chinese Communist Party operatives who were inspired by Sun Yat-sen, the "father of modern China" and one of the originators of the idea of a global development bank. Chinese officials played a role in shaping the proposals for what became the IBRD (or World Bank) at the Bretton Woods Conference in 1944 (Helleiner, 2014, 2019). The People's Republic of China (PRC) assumed the seat of "China" in 1980 and has thereafter joined most of the other "legacy" Multilateral Development Banks (MDBs). Within the legacy MDBs, China was mainly a "rule taker," learning the established rules and norms during the first-two decades (1980s and 1990s),

---

[12] The authors' discussions with UNDP China officials, March 2019.

when it took a significant amount of loans and related forms of development assistance from the MDBs (see Table 5).

But in the last two decades, Beijing has increased its financing and support to the World Bank and the other legacy MDBs. However, it has also sought to make new rules and establish new norms outside of the World Bank (rule-maker), for example, the rules of "moving with speed" on project approvals and directing large amounts of resources to infrastructure development (see Table 5). China has acted according to the new rules both inside China and across the developing world, and it has advanced these new rules either through its own national policy banks, CDB and CHEXIM Bank, or via the two new MDBs that it has helped to launch, the AIIB and the NDB (Chin and Gallagher, 2019). With this combination of inside and outside action, China has also sought to more fundamentally reshape rules inside the World Bank Group and the other legacy MDBs (rule-shaker). At times, other major stakeholders and staff inside the WBG or regional MDBs have undertaken the changes that China has advocated for, as they have felt the pressure of China's growing force both inside and outside of the BWIs, including by trying to shorten the duration for their project approvals and moving more of their investment back into infrastructure (Wilson, 2020).

Despite its evolving behavior, China has had a fairly consistent set of strategic objectives in engaging the WB and the other legacy MDBs that are rooted in its national modernization drive. China's main objectives have been four-fold: first, to overcome capital scarcity, significantly increasing the scale of capital dedicated to national development in order to catalyze major structural transformation; second, to advance a model of development finance that emphasizes infrastructure, industrial transformation, employment creation, and income growth; third,

Table 5 Remaking the Global Development Finance System

	Legacy Order	**Rule-Maker**
Rule-Taker	Joining legacy MDBs	AIIB/NDB
	Competitive bidding	CDB/CHEXIM funding model
	Social and Env standards	
Rule-Shaker	Quota/Capital increases	CDB/CHEXIM credit spaces
	Infrastructure finance	NDB Governance/Local currency lending
	Voice increase	FIC/IDFC
	Conditionality	

to obtain more voice and representation for China (and other developing countries) within global institutions; and fourth, to ensure that China and other developing countries have sufficient policy autonomy to pursue their own national developmental goals and strategies. China has advanced this agenda with one foot inside the legacy MDBs, acting increasingly as an active, generous, and empowered stakeholder, and with one foot outside, constructing a parallel set of multilateral and national institutions outside of the BWIs.

In the last three decades, China has been building a parallel network of development finance institutions (DFIs) that perform similar functions to the World Bank and the legacy MDBs, but they also help to advance China's strategic interests and goals in the global development finance space (see Table 5). At the national level, China has launched two policy banks that have "gone global," namely the CDB and the Export-Import Bank of China (CHEXIM), along with a broad variety of development-oriented equity-based institutions, most notably the Silk Road Fund (SRF). CDB and CHEXIM have matched or exceeded the volume of loans issued by the World Bank from 2008 to 2019. In the past decade, China has also played a formative role in creating two new MDBs: the Asian Infrastructure Investment Bank (AIIB) and the New Development Bank (NDB). Combined, these national DFIs and the two new China-backed MDBs have a loan book that is nearly the size of all the legacy MDBs combined (Chin and Gallagher, 2019).

China as Rule-Taker

The United States and the PRC established official diplomatic relations on January 1, 1979, and the PRC joined the World Bank in 1980. During the first-two decades of its World Bank membership, and after joining the Asian Development Bank, it is well established that China was largely a "rule-taker." China's rule-taking has continued to some degree, but its stance and the outcomes have also evolved into a new "rule-maker" outside of the World Bank and a "rule-shaker" inside the Bank.

For the purposes of this section, we characterize China's "rule-taking" inside the World Bank in three phases. First, as an "exceptional concessional borrower" during the 1980s and 1990s; second, as a "growing, evolving stakeholder" during the first decade of the 2000s; and third, as a "cautious and selective engager." The core of China's discussions inside the World Bank has been over the scale, composition, and target of financing; the preferred development model and policies; the speed of decision-making and delivery of financing; and voice and governance issues.

China's first phase of rule-taking inside the World Bank was one of an "exceptional concessional borrower"; China needed external financial and technical support, and the World Bank saw helping China as a major development challenge of global importance. When then-World Bank President Robert McNamara led a World Bank delegation to China and met with Deng Xiaoping, Deng told the mission, "We are very poor. We have lost touch with the world. We need the World Bank to catch up. We can do it without you, but we can do it quicker and better with you" (Bottelier, 2007, 243). Deng had a national development and reform agenda for China, based on market reforms of the national economy and opening to the outside world, though maintaining a balance between state planning and market dynamics, and the "Four Modernizations," meaning investing to modernize agriculture, industry, military defense, and science and technology, with the latter including improvements in education. China's post-Mao leadership wanted the World Bank's help to accelerate the reforms. China's relations with the World Bank during the first-decades were defined by a fairly consistent agenda, where China absorbed the rules and norms of the World Bank, learned how to operate according to the established rules, and made full use of the World Bank's assistance – financial and technical knowledge – to support China's economic reforms, national modernization, and opening and integration into the world economy. The economic fundamentals – rural development, infrastructure development, industrial modernization, and income growth – were the priorities.

The World Bank took a unique strategic approach to China that combined learning the specifics of China's situation and adapting to what was politically feasible in the PRC case, in providing technical advice and financing. With China, the World Bank was willing to take the approach of a two-way street rather than lead with one-size-fits-all conditionality. When the World Bank first started engaging with China, 97.5 percent of the entire population was living in "poverty" (using the World Bank metric, equivalent to US$2.30 per person per day, 2011); by 2019, it was 0.6 percent – 770 million people had been lifted out of poverty (World Bank, 2022). As an "exceptional concessional borrower," China became a key patron of the Bank in that it became a major borrower from the World Bank, and, in fact, the biggest borrower for a number of years.

For the World Bank, China was both a mammoth undertaking and a huge opportunity. China was (and is) a population giant, and it had a large segment of its people living in poverty. The World Bank had not engaged with Mainland China for more than thirty years. From the early 1980s to the 1990s, China was classified as a "low-income country" and was granted access to the Bank's "soft window" for loans, the International Development Association (IDA). The IDA loans, which China accessed during the 1980s and 1990s, were highly concessional and much more affordable than the Bank's "hard loan window" for middle-income countries, managed by the IBRD. However, China did continue to borrow from the World Bank after its access to the IDA ended in 1999, on less concessional terms.

Uniquely for the World Bank, China's relations with the institution were arguably more of a partnership than patronage (Bottelier, 2007). The partnership dynamics were based on the fact that China was granted an exception to the "shock therapy," "structural adjustment" loans that were the norm for the World Bank during the 1980s and 1990s – a period of deep "neoliberal" or "Washington consensus"-type conditional loans. In contrast, the mode of engagement between China and the World Bank exhibited strong elements of two-way mutual socialization, in that the World Bank learned it had to modify some of its norms and rules in its approach to China if it was to gain a receptive audience for its loans and be effective in transferring its lessons and knowledge to the PRC. More often than not, China and the World Bank would engage in joint technical studies on a priority area or sector for China, which would lead to a series of concessional loans to help address the issues identified in the technical research. For large-scale loans, China was most interested in raising the scale and efficiency of railways, electric power generation and distribution, seaports, inland ports and waterways, highways and bridges, telecommunications, water supply, and water treatment. Operating within these Chinese priorities, the World Bank would introduce its operational norms and standards, such as competitive bidding for projects and third-party validation for engineering and construction efforts, but also its policy norms, such as the role of market forces and market-oriented logic. China, as a rule-taker, internalized these World Bank norms and rules.

From the early 1980s to 1999 (China graduated from IDA in 1999), China received upwards of $10 billion in IDA loans (Bottelier, 2007). During this period, China showed a preference for taking on large-scale World Bank financing for infrastructure, energy, and industrialization projects, where China could exercise its voice as a partner at the negotiating table. In the late 1990s, China also took large-scale loans for environmental protection projects. However, Beijing was largely unwilling to take large-scale loans from the World Bank (or the ADB) for social sector projects in education, health, gender, or social services. The sector allocation of World Bank financing to China during this period was largely a function of the policy control preferences of China's Party-state planners. We highlight that Beijing's sector borrowing choices enabled China to bypass some of the normative and policy preferences of the World Bank – the conditionality that other developing countries had to undertake in order to receive World Bank loans, especially in social policy areas.

This two-way mutual socialization relationship between China and the World Bank (and ADB) from the 1980s to the first-decade of the 2000s contributed to one of the most dramatic national development transformations and modernization stories in world economic history (Hu 2004; World Bank, 2022). During this period, China also created new domestic financial institutions, such as the CDB (in 1994), which have played massive roles in supporting structural transformation and poverty alleviation in China (Chen, 2013). Not to be overlooked, however, are the darker sides of this far-reaching transformation, especially for rural-to-urban migrants, vulnerable workers, inequality, gender disparities, uneven regional development, environmental pollution, and climate damage (Lee, 1998; Solinger, 1999; Hu and Wang, 1999; Khan and Riskin, 2001; Economy, 2004).

China had reached the threshold of what the World Bank defined as a "lower middle-income country" by 1999 and was no longer eligible for IDA loans. China "graduated" to IBRD lower-concessional financing, which, from 2000 to 2020, amounted to upward of $50 billion – more than any other country during that period (Humphrey and Chen, 2021). In the mid-2000s, the World Bank started facing criticism about why it was still providing loans to China. Then-World Bank President Paul Wolfowitz (2005–2007) pushed-back, stating that there were still millions of poor people in China, but he added three new points to the Bank's overall rationale for why it was still active with China:

> First, China still has work to do to help the roughly 150 million people who still live in acute poverty. We can help with money, although we no longer lend on concessional terms; but more important, we can help with ideas and experience. Second, China has a lot to teach the rest of the world. There are lessons of experience – such as the Loess Plateau project that I saw – that are relevant probably to other parts of the world. We can learn and share those lessons. And third, China has an increasingly important role to play as one of the world's major economies. It is providing assistance, and more importantly, it provides inspiration to other developing countries. We need to work together, for the benefit of the poor people of those countries (World Bank, 2005).

Under Wolfowitz's leadership, the World Bank aimed to work with China as a co-donor to help other developing countries by exporting China's success stories, and the Bank also tried to convince China to channel more of its foreign aid financing to, and *through,* the World Bank.

During this period, the World Bank also shifted toward addressing some of the externalities of China's rapid growth in the 1980s and 1990s (Chin, 2014). The World Bank cooperated with the Development Research Center of the State Council on a number of studies on air pollution and climate change, which resulted in the financing of new programs for new technologies and policy support in China (Martinot, 2001; World Bank, 2007). China's rule-taking inside the World Bank in the 2000s involved China adopting the upgraded air quality and clean energy standards of the World Bank, as well as the Bank's own lessons learned by the mid-2000s. As a result of its rule-taking inside the World Bank, China transformed from experiencing difficulty in adopting engineering standards and competitive bidding contracts in its early years in the Bank to Chinese companies being among *the* most competitive bidders for World Bank procurement contracts in the world by the 2000s (Morris, Rockafellow, and Rose, 2021). China's rule-taking inside the World Bank can also be observed in the funding models of CDB and CHEXIM – where paid-in capital is used as collateral to raise funds on capital markets that are on-lent to clients. This approach was co-designed with the World Bank, and remains in use to this day (Bottelier, 2021).

China has become a member of all the major legacy MDBs across the world's regions, from the European Bank for Reconstruction and Development (EBRD) to the Inter-American Development Bank. Figure 2 shows the relative share of Chinese capital contributions and voice ("participation") in each of these institutions. In the World Bank, China is now the third-largest shareholder with a 6 percent voting-share, but it holds a much smaller share in the regional legacy MDBs. The exception is the ADB, where China has a relatively larger voting share, though smaller than the two co-leads, Japan and the US, who have coordinated to block China's efforts at various points. Interestingly, China joined the African Development Bank (AfDB[13]) first, in 1985, and the Asian Development Bank

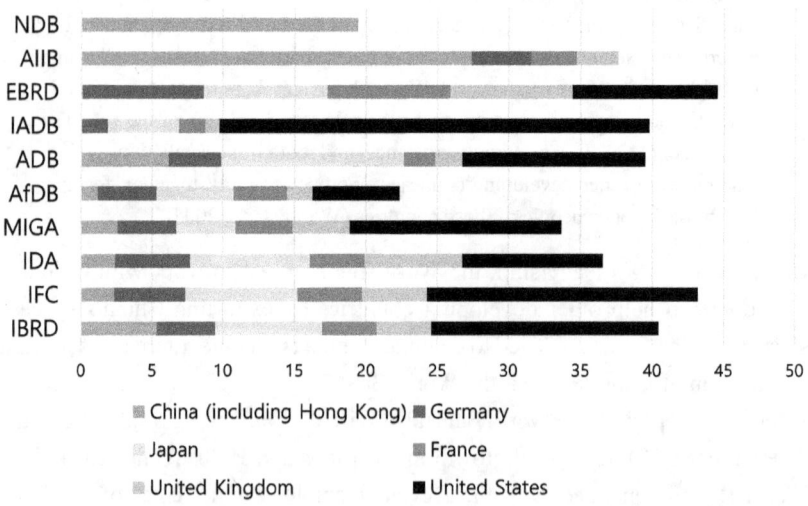

Figure 2 China's capital and voting share in major MDBs

Source: Lee et al., 2023

---

[13] As a vesitage of the past, China is represented by Canada on the Board of Directors of the AfDB.

(ADB) shortly thereafter. China joined the Inter-American Development Bank (IADB) in 2009 and the EBRD in 2009 (Humphrey and Chen, 2021; Morris, Rockafellow, and Rose, 2021). Only in the ADB has China been a borrower, borrowing over $40 billion through 2020 (Humphrey and Chen, 2022).

China as Rule-Maker

By the early 2000s, operating outside of the WBG and the legacy MDBs, China's two state policy banks, both created in 1994 – CDB and CHEXIM – went global. The globalization of CHEXIM and CDB supplied targeted financing for a number of infrastructure projects in Africa and policy lending to China's strategic partners across the Global South, from Asia and Africa to South America and the Caribbean. These two national policy banks also became the beacons of strategic financing for Belt and Road Initiative (BRI) projects after the China-led BRI was launched in 2013.

However, China has been central to the creation of two new MDBs, AIIB and NDB. As Figure 3 shows, by 2020, China's DFIs and the China-backed MDBs had nearly as much equity as all the Western-led legacy MDBs combined. With substantial financial capacity, China could pursue its strategic goals in global development by scaling-up finance, promoting connectivity and infrastructure-led development, and increasing the voice and representation of developing countries and major emerging economies ("Southern countries") in decision-making. Working outside the World Bank and the other established MDBs, China's agenda is to make new rules and norms for global development finance. China's policy banks, along with the AIIB and NDB, are constituent parts of the more diverse multi-polar global development finance scenario that is emerging, where there are now more than 500 development finance institutions outside of the legacy MDB system, with total assets of $20 trillion in 2021, and China has the largest share of that total (Peking University and AFD, 2023).

Figure 3 shows that the China-supported or China's DFIs are close to the size of all the legacy MDBs combined in terms of equity. Indeed, the CDB and CHEXIM are now among the largest development finance institutions in the world in terms of assets. In 2021, the CDB and CHEXIM had combined assets of $3.6 trillion, double the size of the assets of all the legacy MDBs combined. In addition to being active in the BRICS grouping and its broader collective attempts to set common international monetary and global development goals (Roberts, Armijo, and Katada, 2018), China's two policy banks are also participants in the newly created "Finance in Common Summit (FIC)," which brings together the 500-plus development finance institutions in annual summits to coordinate on joint initiatives and common goals, create new rules, and advance

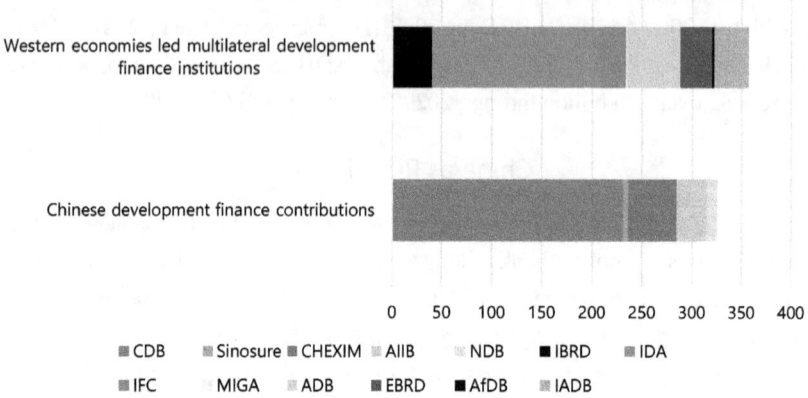

Figure 3 Equity in legacy MDBs and Chinese DFIs
Source: Lee et al., 2023

alternative norms. The FIC aims to be a more inclusive grouping that includes DFIs largely shut out of the annual spring and autumn meetings of the IMF and the World Bank. The FIC publishes joint communiqués and works toward joint efforts. To quote from the 2022 communiqué: "a global go-to platform for all public development banks, promoting increased coherence in their strategies and operations, by accelerating their convergence toward shared standards and best practices. Representing collectively more than 23 trillion US$ of assets and approximately 12% of total global investment each year, it brings together in a concrete and collaborative way key stakeholders from all over the world. Through multilateral fora such as the G20 and the COP, FICS contributes to transform the financial system toward climate, social and sustainability objectives"(Finance in Common, 2022).

Globalization of China's Policy Finance

Similar to the Western-backed MDBs, CDB and CHEXIM had initial paid-in capital (from the People's Bank of China and Ministry of Finance), and they also raised additional financing on capital markets, both onshore and offshore. In just thirty years, these two PRC state policy banks have grown into some of the largest development lenders in the world. CDB is one of the largest development banks in the world, with over US$23 trillion in assets. CDB is wholly owned by various Chinese government shareholders: Ministry of Finance (MOF), 36.54 percent; Central Huijin Investment Ltd. (a subsidiary of the China Investment Corporation, China's sovereign wealth fund), 34.68 percent; Buttonwood Investment Holding Company Ltd. (owned by the State Administration of Foreign Exchange, attached to the central bank), 27.19 per cent; and the National Council for Social Security, 1.59 percent (China Development Bank, 2016). CDB has "ministerial rank" in the government of China and is credited with financing key national and local priority projects from 1994 onward, including in the country's less-developed Central and Western regions. CDB champions "state direction of market development" (Sanderson and Forsythe, 2013; Chen, 2013; Chen, 2024).

CHEXIM's mandate is to "facilitate the export and import of Chinese mechanical and electronic products, complete sets of equipment and new- and high-tech products, assist Chinese companies with comparative advantages in their offshore project contracting and outbound investment, and promote international economic cooperation and trade" (CHEXIM, 2018). CHEXIM achieves these objectives through the provision of export credits, loans to overseas construction and investment projects, and concessional loans. Given the implicit guarantee from the Chinese government, the policy banks can pass on competitive financing to borrowers (Walter and Howie, 2012). Earlier research documented that CDB had a rating of AA-, while CHEXIM was rated A+. CDB's loans were, on average, between 3 and 6 percent, whereas CHEXIM's were 2 to 3 percent, given that some of its loans are blended with grant financing through the Department of Foreign Assistance of the Ministry of Commerce (MOFCOM) as no-interest, highly concessional loans provided by CHEXIM's Department of Preferential Loans (Chen, 2018; Gallagher and Irwin, 2015). CDB also provides foreign investment support, while CHEXIM offers seller's credits to Chinese firms to go global and bid for overseas projects.

Figure 4 compares the lending volumes of China's development institutions with the legacy MDBs. From 2008 until 2019, China's national development

Figure 4 Chinese and World Bank Development Finance, 2008–2021
Source: Global Development Policy Center, 2023

financing was roughly equal to that of the World Bank, though China's development finance tapered during the COVID-19 crisis, and the World Bank reached into buffer funds to meet member needs during the crisis. China's outbound development finance has fallen dramatically since then. Figure 4 shows that Chinese development finance from 2008 to 2021 was $498 billion, compared to the World Bank's $601 billion. Nonetheless, CDB and CHEXIM remain among the largest DFIs in the world.

Table 6 compares the nature of China's state policy banks, the China-backed MDBs, and the legacy MDBs – their budget, organizational, governance, and lending allocation characteristics. It shows how the financing, rules, norms, and models of CDB and CHEXIM are unique. Whereas the Western-backed legacy MDBs conduct individual project financing, China's policy banks take a more *consortium* approach to financing, both at home and abroad, involving bundles of loans or lines of credit for a network of coordinated and corresponding projects, and involving consortia-type groupings of companies and government organizations with shared strategic policy objectives and goals (Chin and Gallagher, 2019). CDB and CHEXIM identify strategic regions or countries, calculating their potential land, mineral, industrialization, and population growth possibilities. This approach can be observed in China's lending to Venezuela, Pakistan, and Turkey, for example, but also in a number of Asian, African, South American, and Caribbean countries. CDB and CHEXIM loans are typically in the billions of dollars, rather than the hundreds of millions typical of MDB financing. The strategy is to trigger a critical mass of economic activity – beyond one single project. Such a broad, coordinated-network credit outlay aims to "crowd in" state commercial banks, Chinese construction and other firms, and local actors into the credit space, with the many beneficiaries (Chin and Gallagher, 2019).

China's Big Four commercial banks provide financing to Chinese (and foreign partner) firms on broadly-classified "development projects" in the borrower countries. Finally, CDB and CHEXIM also support China's foreign aid objectives, at times working in coordination with the Department of Assistance to Foreign Countries in China's Ministry of Commerce (MOFCOM). CDB provides borrowing countries with a variety of non-concessional loans, CHEXIM with concessional loans or no-interest loans, and MOFCOM provides grants. Table 6 and Table 7 contrast Chinese policy banks with their legacy counterparts.

China's two policy banks have created new rules for their development financing. First, related to the aforementioned approach of "coordinated credit," whereby the economic return on investment is estimated across a portfolio of projects rather than the financial return calculated at the project level. One

Table 6 Comparative context of China's DFIs

	Chinese Development Finance	AIIB	NDB	Western MDBs
Scale and Business Model	Paid-in capital	Paid-in capital (& callable capital)	Paid-in capital (&callable capital)	Paid-in capital (& callable capital)
	Bond issuance (China and global market)	Bond issuance (China and global market)	Bond issuance (China and global market)	Bond issuance (Global and local markets)
	Large Scale Deposits	Medium scale	Medium/small scale	Small/Medium scale
	USD and RMB lending	n.a.	n.a.	n.a.
		USD lending	USD and local currency lending	USD and local currency lending
	Coordinated finance	Project finance with competitive bidding	On-lending to NDBs	Project finance with competitive bidding
Composition and approach	Energy and Infrastructure	Energy and Infrastructure	Sustainable Infrastructure	Poverty alleviation, climate change abatement
	Big Push	Big Push	Big Push	Institutionalist/End Growth/ Sen
Governance	Single shareholder	Developing country-led shareholders	Equal shareholders	Industrialized country-led shareholders
	No policy conditionality	No policy conditionality	No policy conditionality	Micro and Macro-level conditionalities
	Country systems ESRM	Conditionally harmonized ESRM	Country systems ESRM	Conditionally harmonized ESRM

Source: Author's adaptation of Chin and Gallagher, 2019

Table 7 China's social and environmental policy in comparison

	Regional DFIs		China DFIs		Peer National DFIs		
	ADB	AIIB	CDB	CHEXIM	DBSA	JICA	JBIC
Preparation							
Exclusion/inclusion lists	X	X		X	X	X	X
Technical support for developing green projects	X	X			X	X	
Financial support for developing green projects	X	X			X	X	
Design							
Use of risk/impact rating system	X	X			X	X	X
Conditions for use of host country standards	X	X	X	X			
Implementation							
Disclosure of lender documents		X				X	X
Facilitation of disclosure of borrower documents	X	X			X	X	
Use of independent/third-party monitors	X	X			X		
Operation and Completion							
Project completion provisions	X	X	X	X	X		
Independent accountability mechanism	X	X			X	X	X

Note: ADB: Asian Development Bank; AIIB: Asian Infrastructure Investment Bank; DBSA: Development Bank of Southern Africa; JICA: Japan International Cooperation Agency; JBIC: Japan Bank for International Cooperation.

Source: Adapted from Guo, Gallagher, and Zhang, 2022.

example is how CDB made the fulfillment of a railway network project in Argentina cross-conditional on the fulfillment of two hydro-electric power dams in a remote mountainous area of the country (Patey, 2017). Second, China's state banks sometimes secure their overseas development loans by backing them with the option to be repaid in commodities, natural resources, or energy supplies from the borrower-country instead of cash (Brautigam and Gallagher, 2014). In the case of some African countries, China has offered such commodity-backed-loans. These practices and the associated rules diverge from the established rules of the legacy MDBs.

The determinants of Chinese overseas development finance are a combination of supply ("push") and demand ("pull") factors (Kong and Gallagher, 2020; Li et al., 2021). The major push factor is China's massive current account surplus that gives China a supply of low yielding US dollars and China's desire to globalize its firms, first as part of the "Going Out" and then the BRI strategies (Chin and Helleiner, 2008; Gallagher et al., 2023). Other factors are overcapacity in industries that are powerful and looking for overseas expansion, and the need to secure strategic imports such as transition materials and petroleum (Li et al, 2022; Dreher et al. 2022; Gallagher et al., 2023). The main pull factors are enormous infrastructure finance gaps and needs of the borrower countries, their limited options for external finance, and their policy goals and priorities (Li et al., 2022).

China's overseas development finance (ODF) has brought significant benefits to the borrowers but has also accentuated risks. China's development finance is strongly associated with economic growth, whereas World Bank projects are not (Dreher et al., 2022; Ruta et al., 2019; Mandon and Woldemichael, 2023). China's ODF has eased medium-term liquidity constraints and given developing countries more options for financing (Sundquist, 2021; Kaplan, 2021). However, Chinese development finance is also associated with potential risks, especially social and environmental. Table 7 shows that the standards of China's state policy banks are different from legacy MDBs such as the ADB, and even the AIIB. A significant proportion of China's overseas development finance has gone to financing fossil fuel power plants and has been associated with biodiversity risk (Chen et al., 2021; Yang et al., 2021).

Present at the Creation: China and the New MDBs

Alongside China's two globalized national policy banks, Beijing has also played a major role in creating two multilateral development banks, NDB and AIIB. These new MDBs do have what could be called "China's characteristics," but they also resemble legacy MDBs in a number of respects. The NDB –

created by Brazil, Russia, India, China, and South Africa (the BRICS) – opened its Head Office in Shanghai in December 2015, and the NDB and AIIB have been pursuing "new ways of doing things" on a number of fronts, with regard to new norms, rules, policies, and standards, and succeeding to varying degrees (Chin, 2019, 2024; Hofman and Srinivas, 2024).

Some of the most explicit rule changes that the AIIB and the NDB are advancing are in their approaches to operations and lending (the business or work of the banks), such as moving with speed on project approvals and directing large amounts of development finance to sustainable infrastructure, energy, especially renewables, new industrialization, economic growth, and income generation, rather than basic education and basic health for the "poorest of the poor," for example. Again, the senior management of these China-supported new MDBs are aware of the frustrations of developing countries, large and small, about the slow speed of the World Bank, for example, on project approvals and the complexity of the procedures (see for example Maasdorp, 2019).

AIIB President Jin Liqun describes the AIIB as a "21st Century development bank," saying that it was "clear from the start that the greatest need across the developing world was in the field of infrastructure." He adds, "The idea was to create a bank that would help Asian countries but also boost global connectivity and trade" (quoted in Wilson, 2020). A senior official at a rival regional MDB depicts the AIIB's rule-making character as such: "It [AIIB] was set up as a multilateral for infrastructure financing. It is not a development bank in the strictest sense of the word." AIIB Vice President of Policy and Strategy Joachim von Amsberg states that the AIIB is partially a "development bank" as the Bank "has a development mandate," but it is also an infrastructure bank "as we finance infrastructure," and an investment bank "as we mobilize investment" – "we are all three" (Wilson, 2020). The AIIB's new norm-setting for MDBs and development finance is captured in Jin's two iconic statements that the AIIB's operational structure is "flat, lean, agile," and the Bank's overall motto is "clean, lean and green," that is, corruption-free, cost and operational efficiency, and committed to sustainability and delivering on the Paris climate agenda. Jin remarked, "From the start we set out to be a new type of institution that learned from others while innovating and creating our own products and services" (Wilson, 2020). The official from the other regional MDB acknowledged: "To give them credit, their rules make them a bit more efficient than us" (Wilson, 2020).

The NDB and AIIB have been largely modeled on the legacy MDBs, for example, with their funding model of raising financing on global capital markets for project loans and competitive bidding procurement processes. However, both China-backed new MDBs have sought to move beyond US dollar financing and lending, which has been the rule and norm of the BWIs for much of their existence. NDB and, more recently, AIIB have pioneered the use of local currency for their fund raising and lending operations, particularly the use of China's RMB for bond issues and project loans. Both China-supported MDBs, especially the NDB, have been trend setters by raising additional financing in local currencies on onshore and offshore capital markets. In July 2016, NDB issued its first bonds, "green RMB," in China's onshore interbank bond markets – a RMB 3 billion (US$ 450 million) bond sale with a 5-year tenor. The NDB released its first set of financing packages for green, clean renewable energy projects in 2016 in the five founding member-countries, which were largely financed from the RMB green bond. It has returned to China's interbank bond market four more times, issuing a total of RMB 47.5 billion in "panda bonds" by February 2024. Although the majority of NDB's financial operations and fund-raising are in US dollars, it has used local currencies for 22 percent, including for on-lending in local currency, and it has committed to a target of 30 percent local currency use for the work period 2022–2026, which is unique among the MDBs. In August 2023, NDB issued its first rand bonds in Johannesburg, South Africa, and there is much talk of NDB issuing Indian rupee bonds.

NDB members had previously committed that 60 percent of their project lending would be allocated to renewable energy projects. In 2021, NDB members agreed that 40 percent of the Bank's project funding for 2022–2026 would be dedicated to projects focused on "climate change mitigation and adaptation, and supporting member countries to transition to a more sustainable development path" (NDB, 2022). Additionally, aiming to establish new norms and rules of South-South cooperation, NDB founders agreed that, rather than imposing external standards on their developing country partners, such as the one-size-fits-all approach to rules of traditional Northern development lenders, the NDB does not attach political or policy conditionalities to its financing. Similar to China's DFIs, CDB and CHEXIM, NDB has adopted the rule of a "country systems approach" (i.e., borrowing country regulations) to environmental and social standards and safeguards on its loans.

Initially, the AIIB largely co-financed projects with other MDBs, starting with the World Bank and ADB in particular, and it relied on the ESG standards of the legacy MDBs for its loans within these co-financed projects. However, on environmental and social standards, the AIIB has shifted away from the World Bank and its initial reliance on the safeguards of the legacy MDBs, pushing to improve upon the legacy MDBs (Lichenstein, 2018; Humphrey, 2023). Similar to the NDB, the AIIB has stated that it will not attach policy conditionalities to its loans for borrowing governments. From 2019 to 2021, AIIB members worked on revising its own "Environment and Social Framework" (ESF) and issued the revised version in May 2021. The goal of AIIB members under its revised ESF is to exceed the "best practices" of the legacy MDBs – in other words, not just new standards but better standards, rules, and norms outside of the World Bank. The AIIB has also developed an "energy framework" that is linked to members' elevated climate and carbon-neutral commitments after signing the Paris Climate Agreement. The AIIB has committed to directing a substantial portion of its financing to renewable energy. Additionally, the AIIB has pledged to only finance coal-fired power plants under certain circumstances, aiming to articulate new norms and rules for limiting its support for non-renewables.

The NDB has also advanced new governance and representational rules and norms. In contrast to the rule of weighted representation in the IMF and World Bank, each founding BRICS member contributed an equal share toward establishing the start-up capital of US$50 billion (i.e., US$10 billion each), with another US$50 billion as callable capital, for a total of US$100 billion (Chin, 2014). The equal contribution rule was, in turn, linked to the rule of equal voice (20 percent voting-share each). Another related new rule was that the BRICS member countries would always hold a minimum of 55 percent voting power, split five ways equally, even as more members joined in the future. These governance rules are unique to the NDB. Also distinct from the rules of the BWIs, with their resident boards, the BRICS governments also agreed to a non-resident board of governors and a non-resident board of directors to supervise the senior management team.

The NDB's governance rules stand in contrast with the established MDBs, whereby ownership and voting are dominated by industrialized countries, usually not the borrowers, and where voting shares are weighted according to paid-in capital and the size of the member's economy. Wanting to draw a contrast, the BRICS nations agreed instead to grant each founding member equal voting power in the NDB, regardless of the size of their economy, on the understanding that each member state would match the rest with their capital contributions. Also to make a break from the rules and norms of the BWIs, which have a long-established precedent of appointing IMF Managing Directors from Europe and the World Bank Presidents from the USA, the NDB founders established a pre-ordained rotating presidency and vice presidencies among the five BRICS founders. Moreover, the NDB has a rule that when developed countries join the NDB (e.g., the UAE), as a group they are limited to a 20 percent maximum voting share and would join the Bank as "non-borrowing members." Other developing countries join as "borrowing members" (e.g., Bangladesh, Egypt, and, still pending, Uruguay), and they hold smaller shares than the founders.

AIIB has more organizational characteristics that are similar to the legacy Western-led MDBs than NDB, but there are some other differences that also stand-apart from the BWIs in its governance arrangements and its handling of environmental and social standards. AIIB was initially created to support infrastructure construction inside the Asian region, but its membership expanded rapidly into every continent, and it has become a "global" MDB with 110 "full members" by 2024. AIIB was proposed by China in 2013 and formally started operations in January 2016 after the Articles of Agreement (AoA) entered into force with ratification from 17 member states holding 50.1 percent of the shares (Chin, 2019). The quota and voting structure of the AIIB is derived from the Western-MDB model (Lichenstein, 2018). However, AIIB's non-resident dual boards – a non-resident Board of Governors and Board of Directors – above the senior management team are similar to NDB, and different from the Western-led MDBs, which have resident Boards of Directors (Chin, 2016). But on voting share, similar to the legacy MDBs, each member of AIIB's boards holds a differing and specified share of voting power that is determined by their differing amounts of capital paid into the bank. In AIIB, China is the dominant shareholder, holding 26.6 percent of the votes, which gives China veto power. In this regard, China's status in AIIB is similar to that of the United States in the Bretton Woods institutions and the Inter-American Development Bank.

China as Rule-Shaker

China's interventions to shake up or re-shape the rules inside the World Bank trace back at least as far as the late-1990s. In the aftermath of the 1997–1998 Asian financial crisis, China's finance minister, Xiang Huaicheng, as China's Governor to the World Bank, called on the Bank at the September 1999 Annual Meetings in Washington, DC, to increase its concessional lending for poverty reduction in low-income countries and to keep out of the domestic politics of the borrowing countries, such as pushing particular "good governance" models in East Asia:

> At present when the economy of crisis-affected countries has generally restored stability, the Bank should shift its focus back to address the long-term development issues still facing developing countries, particularly poverty reduction. We [China] hope the Bank ... will build upon its comparative advantages to provide more concessional funds and further promote the capital flow to its developing country members. We also hope the Bank will

strictly keep its political neutrality in the conduct of its business and resist any attempts to politicize the Bank (IMF, 1999).

The finance minister added one further caution, if not criticism, of the World Bank's emerging emphasis on social sector lending across the developing world: "We [China] have also noted the increased emphasis put on social sector issues by the two institutions [World Bank and IMF]. We believe that economic development is a precondition to solutions to poverty alleviation and social issues." China's representatives registered their preference for the older economic growth-based developmental agenda, anchored on industrial development, employment growth, and infrastructure, in contrast to the "pro-poor poverty reduction-focused" agenda of the World Bank in the late-1990s and early 2000s. To quote Xiang: "The two institutions should help developing countries achieve stable and steady growth, which in turn will help reduce poverty and solve social issues."

By the early 2000s, other developing countries perceived China as the major developmental success story of the 1980s and 1990s; and China was amassing an increasingly large foreign currency reserve, which it could use to provide credit to others. The World Bank, the UN, and the other MDBs were all aware that China and the other "BRIC" countries were growing rapidly, and that China especially was turning into the world's leading trading power and foreign investor in Africa and Asia. From 2003–2004 onward, the UN Secretary-General Kofi Annan and his special advisor on the MDGs, Jeffrey Sachs, invited China's leaders to increase their country's contributions to the MDGs, and to offer China's own experiences, its development lessons, and its science and technology in the medical sciences and agriculture to other developing countries. China's President Hu Jintao and Premier Wen Jiabao stepped up, cautiously, to offer China's medicines and technical know-how, as well as its own development experiences, for other developing countries to examine and draw their own lessons (Chin, 2023).

As detailed above, from the mid-2000s onward, the World Bank senior management increasingly pressed China to work more with the World Bank as a co-donor and to increase its contributions to the Bank. China's profile within the World Bank grew when Bank President Robert Zoellick (2007–2012) urged China to further increase its financial contributions to the World Bank, and China agreed. Zoellick recognized China's growing presence outside the World Bank as a financier of international development, and he called on China to be a "responsible stakeholder" within the BWIs. In return, Zoellick supported the appointment of Justin Yifu Lin as the Chief Economist and Senior Vice President of the World Bank, commencing in June 2008. This marked a first for a PRC-national, and for the developing world, and signified the US President George W. Bush Administration's acknowledgment of China's growing weight and profile in the world. The appointment was also a response to Beijing's desire to be "appropriately recognized" within the major global economic governance institutions.

The effects of *China's two-way countervailing power*, rule-shaking, and re-shaping within the World Bank were further exemplified when Zoellick supported Bank staff in putting together a Memorandum of Understanding with CHEXIM Bank in 2007 to further strengthen the "partnership" between the World Bank and China's state policy banks, including their mutually agreed intention to initiate some new co-financing projects in African countries. Another example of the countervailing effect was the United States relenting to Beijing's push (along with that of the BRICS) to change the rules on the balance of representation in the Bank membership, when the US and Zoellick supported the increase in China's shares and voice in April 2010, making China the third largest shareholder in the World Bank, overtaking large European nations (Germany, Britain, and France) and ranking behind only the US and Japan.

Also, at the G20 Leaders' summits, China and BRICS members India and Brazil, along with Asian and African governments, criticized the "MDB family," particularly the World Bank, for not providing enough financing for infrastructure development and modernization in the developing world, being too slow with its decision-making on infrastructure projects, and making its environmental and social impact standards too onerous. China's leaders and officials could leverage their own successes as infrastructure financiers outside of the World Bank and the other MDBs to push the World Bank to provide more infrastructure investment to developing countries, and WB staff and Western governments were also conscious of China's "outside" achievements. The criticism on infrastructure coalesced at the G20 Leaders' Summit in Seoul, Korea, in November 2010, and infrastructure investment was listed as the first priority in the action agenda in the G20's "Seoul Declaration," which called for more infrastructure investment from the MDBs in the developing world. China's senior leaders and senior officials continued to call on the MDBs to provide more infrastructure investment at successive G20 summits and other forums.

In the second decade of the 2000s, during Kim's presidency of the World Bank (2012–2019), China further increased its support for the World Bank's green agenda. Recognizing Kim's interest in promoting green initiatives, Beijing focused on pushing the World Bank to innovate and increase its investment in *sustainable* infrastructure. Citing China's leadership in infrastructure globally, Kim did increase infrastructure investment again across the World Bank Group, launching the "billions to trillions" mantra to combine various lines of finance and better meet infrastructure demand across the developing world. Kim was also very aware of the reality that China was adding to its support for investment outside of the World Bank and the established MDBs by creating the AIIB and the NDB, and how China and its partners succeeded in launching these new MDBs within a three-year period. As another example of two-way countervailing influence, it is noteworthy that Kim, as World Bank president, did not oppose the creation of the AIIB or the NDB, and he even directed the World Bank to support the new AIIB by agreeing to co-finance some of the AIIB's first projects, which helped the China-backed new MDB to get off the ground and running (Chin and Gallagher, 2019; Chin, 2019).

China's shake-up of the World Bank and its countervailing effects can also be observed in how the World Bank (and the other legacy MDBs) have agreed to expand the scale of their lending, move more rapidly with their project approvals process, shift back to financing more infrastructure projects, consider supporting new industrialization, remove some of their conditionalities, and reconsider the role of industrial policy and state direction of economic development. In addition, more voice has been given to China and other developing countries inside the Bank (see Table 7). These elements have not been the policy or programming norms in the legacy MDBs since the early 1980s (*the* exception may be the ADB), when their focus moved to structural adjustment and Washington Consensus policies and norms, such as pulling the state out of economic activity and letting static price dynamics determine sectors of focus and specialization (Humphrey, 2022).

In 2006, among the legacy MDBs, there was growing concern about the impacts of China's rise as an overseas development financier, particularly through the China Export-Import Bank and the China Development Bank, whose loans were seen as undercutting the World Bank (and IMF) in a number of instances. For example, in that year, the World Bank was considering suspending a loan to Chad on the claim that Chad had broken a pact to use oil revenue to fight poverty. However, China's banks made a counteroffer, and this weakened the leverage of the World Bank in its attempt to influence Chadian policy (Chin, 2014).

China's rule-shaking within the World Bank in recent years, tracing back to the 2008–09 Global Financial Crisis (GFC), has occurred with China acting as a more "cautious engager" compared to its approach from 1980 to the GFC. By 2015, China had reached another World Bank milestone of "Graduation Discussion Income," where its income level was considered above the threshold to "graduate" from IBRD financing as well (roughly $7,000 GDP per capita at the time). The relationship between China and the World Bank has become more strained, and one can observe the beginning of pushback from traditional Western powers, particularly the United States, against China's efforts to exercise countervailing power in its rule-shaking within the BWIs. For example, Beijing has sought the World Bank's support for Chinese President Xi Jinping's signature foreign policy initiative, the Belt and Road Initiative (BRI). Chinese authorities hoped the World Bank would support the BRI not only through financing and investment but also by pulling in the other legacy Multilateral Development Banks (MDBs) and by helping China and BRI partner countries figure out how to maximize the benefits and minimize the risks of the BRI. President Kim attended the first Belt and Road Forum for International Cooperation (BRI Summit) in May 2017. Toward the end of his term, Kim (2018–2019) created a group within the Bank to "study" the BRI and explore possible roles for the World Bank. The World Bank's research in 2019 found that the potential benefits of the BRI could be upward of 3 percent of GDP, which is twice as large as the US-led Trans-Pacific Partnership (TPP) that partly triggered the inception of the BRI (World Bank, 2019; Ye, 2020). The research group also assessed the potential risks of the BRI, including debt distress, public procurement challenges, and environmental and social risks (World Bank, 2019).

However, by 2018, as Kim was preparing to depart the WB presidency, the Bank started to look for ways to reduce its involvement in the BRI, but not to make it obvious. In 2018, China initiated the Multilateral Cooperation Center for Development Finance (MCDF) meetings to try to corral the MDBs to support the BRI. The World Bank agreed to join the meetings together with other MDBs and China's financial ministry. At these discussions, Chinese authorities pressed the MDBs to determine how they would contribute to the BRI. The World Bank signed two MOUs that committed the MCDF partners to work further, but the World Bank avoided taking on a leading role within the MCDF. The next World Bank president, David Malpass (2019–2023), nominated by US President Donald Trump, directed the Bank to take a more arm's-length stance toward China and especially the BRI. As Donald Trump's Under Secretary for the Treasury for International Affairs, Malpass had criticized the BRI in public statements, and he brought the WB's involvement in the BRI to a halt after becoming Bank president.

Moreover, the WBG started to increase its investment once again in infrastructure. WB figures show that the new trend in infrastructure investment rose from early 2010s onward, with a surge in 2022. To make the point about the need to return to economic fundamentals directly within the legacy MDBs where it is a member, China has even created dedicated co-financed funds for infrastructure financing and industry support within the legacy MDBs: $2 billion with IADB, $2 billion with AfDB, and $3 billion with the IFC (Humphrey and Chen, 2021, 16).

Qualitative interviews with World Bank staff reaffirm the operation of countervailing power. Zeitz (2021) details that legacy MDBs were presented with the choice to either "emulate or differentiate" in response to China's increased lending, and she performs a multi-country regression analysis comparing Chinese and World Bank development projects in more than 100 countries. Zeitz finds that the World Bank is more an emulator than a differentiator: the World Bank has shifted to allocating a greater share of its project finance to infrastructure after developing countries started receiving more Chinese development finance. Zeitz further observes that China is "shaping the type of development that donors support [at both the global and subnational level] by introducing bottom-up competitive pressure" (Zeitz, 2021, p. 265). In another study, Hernandez (2021), based on econometric analysis of panel data for fifty-four African countries between 1980 and 2013, finds that the World Bank approved loans with significantly fewer conditionalities in countries that also received loans from China: 15 percent fewer conditionalities for every percentage-point increase in Chinese development finance.

4 China and the Future of the Bretton Woods Order

This Element has shown how China and its counterparts in the Global South have been able to advance many of their strategic goals within the Bretton Woods order. China now has a seat at the table of the major MDBs and the IMF, its currency has been added as a component of the SDR basket, and it has played a key role in easing conditionalities and pressures for capital account liberalization. These successes were a function of China's persistent push for changes, its leveraging of the West's interest in including China in the rules-based system, its efforts in building internal coalitions at the BWIs on the inside, and its creation of an apparatus of alternative institutions that serve similar functions to the BWIs on the outside. Such a strategy has allowed China to protect and project its own domestic and foreign economic policy interests, create more choices for countries in the Global South, and support the transition to a broader, more multi-layered, and multipolar order of development finance institutions, crisis liquidity, monetary, and reserve options.

Throughout this Element, we have shown how the size of China's economy, its growing global economic weight and reach, its absorption of the established norms, rules, and standards of the BWIs, and Beijing's role in supporting the

Table 8 China and the Global Economic Order

	Monetary System	**Development Finance System**	**Enchancing Chinese Objectives**
Rule-Taker	US dollar	Legacy MDB member	Accelerated learning and integration into financial and monetary system
	IMF member	Socialized norms	Recipient of financing and advice on development priorities
	Financial socialization		"Stamp of approval" for confidence from Western Investment
Rule-Maker	RMB Internationalization	CDB/CHEXIM/ Equity Funds	Expands use of RMB for trading and liquidity finance
	PBOC liquidity swaps	AIIB/NDB	Builds bilateral and multilateral sources of capital for cevelopment
	CDB liquidity loans	Belt Road Initiative	Expands regional and global alliances of countervailing power
	CMIM/CRA		
Rule-Shaker	SDR issuances	Capital Increases/ Voice reform	IMF and WB that is more expansionary without conditionalities
	RMB in SDR basket	Shift to infrastructure	Policy space for Chinese capital account policy and positions
	IMF capital account policy	lessening of World Bank conditionality	Shift of financing toward infrastructure-led development
	IMF quota reform		More voice for China and other countries in Global South

creation of parallel institutions have involved China taking up a unique position as a rule-taker, rule-maker, and rule-shaker in the international monetary and financial systems. Table 8 summarizes some of the key areas where China has been a taker, maker, and shaker of global rules in the monetary and development finance realms, and the extent to which those changes were part of China's strategic objectives.

By joining the BWIs as a rule-taker, China accelerated learning and integration into the global financial and monetary system, which helped China gain a stamp of approval, a seat at the global table, and facilitated surges of investment and trade with the rest of the world. China also remade many of the rules in the system through the creation of new institutions and arrangements in both the monetary and development finance realms – offering new levels of financing bilaterally, regionally, and at the global multilateral level through the BRICS institutions. In some cases, though not all, China offered new institutions and introduced new norms in some of these institutions. As discussed throughout the volume, China and many countries in the Global South have fundamental concerns with the BWIs' insistence on conditionality requirements such as fiscal consolidation, social and environmental regulation, capital account liberalization, and Western veto power and Executive Head position privileges in the legacy BWIs. They have pushed instead for Global South countries to have more voice and representation, and for more emphasis to be given to sustainable infrastructure and new industrialization over free markets. With some exceptions, the China-backed institutions do not impose economic, governance, environmental, or social conditions onto member countries (there are implicit geopolitical conditions such as adherence to the "One China" policy), and they are not built on the asymmetric governance structures of the legacy BWIs. The two-way leveraging of influence has helped China to advance changes in some of the rules and norms within the BWIs. For example, IMF and World Bank voting arrangements have become slightly more equitable through quota and capital increases between North and South, the IMF has moderated its capital account opening norms and rules, and the World Bank has given more priority and resources to infrastructure, with less conditionality.

In the short century thus far, China's hybrid positioning – joining the BWIs and legacy MDBs and building a series of alternative institutions that perform similar functions – and its exertion of two-way countervailing power have enabled China to gain more influence within the global economic system. By the end of the first quarter of the twenty-first century, China no longer needs the BWIs as much as it did in the 1980s and 1990s, especially the World Bank Group. However, even though China has learned and absorbed many of the norms, rules, and standards from the IMF, and has formed its own safety nets and development finance providers such that China has gone a certain distance in becoming a new lender of last resort to other countries, China arguably still needs the IMF to exist, to act as the main global crisis liquidity provider for the many developing countries of the world, but also possibly to help if China ever becomes engulfed by a serious economic crisis.

Can China's reform drives inside the BWIs and outside be sustained, especially if Western powers, principally the United States, choose to confront China on its reform efforts? There are clear signs that such opposition to China's efforts to change the rules and norms is already underway and has become the norm for the United States inside the World Bank. For example, in 2018, during the Trump presidency, the US opposed a large capital increase in the World Bank and China's offer to increase its capital contribution to the World Bank, which would have resulted in another increase in China's voice in the Bank. China had successfully lobbied for two capital increases at the World Bank during the first decade of the 2000s that brought increases in China's voting share. For the 2010 increase, China worked with the BRICS countries to push for capital and voice rule changes and gained the support of the Barack Obama administration (Roberts, 2018). World Bank President Robert Zoellick stated that the 2010 voice reforms were "crucial for the Bank's legitimacy" (quoted in Chin, 2014, 183). But in 2018, US–China relations had worsened under US President Donald Trump, and the administration resisted, leading the World Bank membership to agree only to a small increase in China's capital contribution to the World Bank. 2019 marked a further turning-point in US–China relations at the World Bank. Malpass, as Bank President, reflected President Trump's more confrontational approach to US–China relations, and that of the US Congress.

China's general approach of cautious engagement with the WB continued under the administration of Joseph Biden, which proposed a series of significant WB reforms to shift the focus of the institution onto Global Public Goods (GPGs), such as addressing climate change and pandemics. Such an approach required a change in the WB's mission to include climate change and an adjustment to the WB's country-demand-led model, which was key to China's strong engagement with the WB, to a more non-borrower-led provision based on the need to provide global public goods (Morris, 2023). China joined a group of the Bank's borrowing members from the developing world to resist this approach, concerned that it would weaken the voice of developing countries in favor of Western priorities. China and its partners countered that a more appropriate solution would be to expand the capital base of the WB to help countries meet their own national development strategies and provide more global public goods, rather than shift the existing capital toward such ends. China also noted that such capital increases would require a reallocation of voting shares within the WB, likely to the detriment of the voice of developing countries. During his term, which stretched into the first few years of the Joseph Biden administration, Malpass accused China of being a major contributor to the debt buildup and for not offering debt relief. This response from the WB president infuriated Beijing, which pushed back, arguing that while China held 7 percent of developing country debt, the WB and other MDBs held 18 percent and were not offering to take a "haircut" at all. Both the WB and China eventually joined the Global Sovereign Debt Round Table, the forum led by the IMF – not the WB – that sought to work on a solution (Gallagher, 2022).

In 2019, US pushback on China also spilled over into China's engagement with the Inter-American Development Bank (IADB). China was set to host the 75th anniversary of the IADB, and the Bank was set to unveil a number of cooperative financing arrangements with China at the anniversary ceremonies. However, the Trump administration insisted that representatives of the Venezuelan opposition party – which the US had worked to ensure were recognized by the IADB – represent Venezuela, rather than the Nicolás Maduro-led government. When China denied the political opposition a foreign visitor visa, the US pushed the IADB members to agree to cancel the meetings that China would have hosted (Bernstein, 2020). Soon thereafter, the US appointed Mauricio Claver-Carone as IADB President with the explicit plan for the IADB to supplant Chinese lending in the region, which had surpassed IADB lending for some years. Although Claver-Carone was ousted in 2022 on ethics and misconduct charges (Stott, 2022), this was another episode of direct US rebuttals against China's growing influence in the global development finance realm. Under the Biden administration, the WB continued to resist calls from Beijing and across the developing world for further capital increases in the WB and the other MDBs and instead backed new Western-led initiatives such as the Partnership for Global Infrastructure Investment as rivals to the BRI (Moses and Zhu, 2022).

Western lawmakers have also tried to roll back China's growing influence as a development financier and crisis liquidity provider by pushing the US Administration to intervene via the IMF. During the Trump presidency, US Senators attempted to bring the US–China tensions into the IMF by proposing to the Executive Branch of the US government that it should prevent the IMF from providing any lender-of-last-resort financing to nations that have accepted financing from China for Belt and Road projects. In August 2018, sixteen US Senators wrote to Treasury Secretary Steven Mnuchin and Secretary of State Michael Pompeo, urging the Trump administration to block the IMF from bailing out countries that had accepted BRI project loans. They named the countries of Pakistan, Sri Lanka, and Djibouti, referred to "predatory Chinese infrastructure financing," and accused Beijing of using such financing to control other countries. In an interview with CNBC, Secretary Pompeo stated enthusiastically that Washington was tracking potential scenarios: "Make no mistake, we will be watching what the IMF does. There's no rationale for US tax dollars ... to go to bail out Chinese bond holders or China itself." Edwin Truman, a longtime and key former US Treasury insider over many US presidential administrations, warned that such moves are an "ominous new front" opening in the rivalry between the US and China for dominance in the IMF, which ultimately damages the IMF itself (Truman, 2018). Truman called, instead, for the "future of the IMF" to be put high on the agenda for US–China talks, but he was not optimistic that such enlightened reason would prevail. Under the Biden presidency, the US Administration took a "one step forward, one step backward" approach to the demand from China and Global South countries for quota increases after the COVID crisis. On the one hand, the United States and other major Western shareholders acquiesced to a quota increase in 2023, which increased the IMF's resources, but on the other hand, the US and its allies made the unprecedented insistence that the quota increase be "equiproportional," which meant that the quota increase would not coincide with a re-alignment of quota and voting shares. So although the objective of increasing the financial firepower of the IMF was achieved, this happened without meeting the other objective of Beijing and its Global South partners: expanding their voice and representation inside the Fund.

For those who wish the centrality of the BWIs to continue (such as Morris, 2023, p. 387), the hopeful path would see the United States, as the IMF and WB's largest shareholder, and China, rising to number two, embracing a more cooperative mode of interaction globally, both inside the BWIs and outside. The United States would need to welcome new links between the China-supported institutions, the new rules, and the BWIs. But for this more cooperative orientation to emerge or prevail, a new understanding would need to be established between the US, China, and the main powers in the legacy institutions, where each sees the BWIs as *the* main institutions to provide the five core global public goods identified by Kindleberger and discussed in the first section. This would entail mutual respect for the other's interests and positions in the IMF and WB, as well as outside, and agreement to work toward a more ambitious future institutional reform agenda. This Element goes to press as the administration of the second Donald Trump presidency is putting its stamp on the office in 2025. Beijing's strategy of two-way countervailing power will certainly be put to the test. While this approach has served Beijing well in the past, it remains to be seen what the future holds.

References

Acharya, Amitav (2017). After Liberal Hegemony: The Advent of a Multiplex World Order, Ethics and International Affairs.

Alacevich, Michele (2011). The World Bank and the Politics of Productivity: The Debate on Economic Growth, Poverty, and Living Standards in the 1950s. *Journal of Global History.* 6(1), 53–74.

Alden, Chris and Vieira, Marco (2005). The New Diplomacy of the South: South Africa, Brazil, India and Trilateralism. *Third World Quarterly,* 26(7), 1077–1095.

Andrews, David (1994). *International Monetary Power.* Ithaca: Cornell University Press.

Andrews, David (2006). *International Monetary Power.* Ithaca: Cornell University Press.

ASEAN+3 Macroeconomic Research Office (AMRO) (2023). About Us: Supporting RFAs and the Implementation of the CMIM, *AMRO,* https://amro-asia.org/about-us/regional-financing-arrangements/.

ASEAN+3. (2005). The Joint Ministerial Statement of the 8th ASEAN+3 Finance Ministers' Meeting, Istanbul, Turkey, *ASEAN,* May 4, https://asean.org/the-joint-ministerial-statement-of-the-8th-asean3-finance-ministers-meeting-istanbul-turkey/.

Asian Development Bank (ADB) (2009). Enhancing ADB's Response to the Global Economic Crisis: Establishing the Countercyclical Support Facility, *ADB Policy Paper,* May, www.adb.org/documents/enhancing-adbs-response-global-economic-crisis-establishing-countercyclical-support.

Barma, Naazneen, Ratner, Ely and Weber, Steven (2007). A World without the West. *The National Interest,* 90, 23–30.

Barnett, Michael, and Finnemore, Martha (2004). *Rules for the World: International Organizations in Global Politics.* Cornell University Press.

Batista Jr., Paulo Nogueira (2021). *BRICS and the Financing Mechanisms They Created.* London: Anthem Press.

Bernstein, Ben (2020). Trump's Pick for Latin Bank Wants to Counter China Influence, *Bloomberg News,* August 26. www.bloomberg.com/news/articles/2020-08-26/trump-candidate-for-latin-bank-wants-to-counter-china-influence.

Bluestein, Paul (2012, 22 June). A Flop and a Debacle; Inside the IMF's Global Rebalancing Act. *CIGI Papers,* (4).

Boston University Global Development Policy Center (2023). China's Overseas Development Finance Database.

Bottelier, Pieter (2007). China and the World Bank: How a Partnership Was Built. *Journal of Contemporary China*, 16(51), 239–258.

Bottelier, Pieter (2021). *Chinese Economic Policy-Making*. London: Routledge.

Brautigam, Deborah and Gallagher, Kevin (2014). Bartering Globalization: China's Commodity-Backed Finance in Africa and Latin America. *Global Policy*, 5, 3.

Bremmer, Ian (2012). *Every Nation for Itself: Winners and Loser in a G-Zero World*. New York: Portfolio.

Chen, Muyang (2018). "Official Aid or Export Credit?". Boston University, Global Development Policy Center, GCI Working Paper 001/06. www.bu.edu/gdp/files/2018/07/GCI-Muyang-Chen-2018.pdf.

Chen, Muyang. (2024). *The Latecomer's Rise: Policy Banks and the Globalization of China's Development Finance*. Ithaca: Cornel University Press.

Chen, Xu, Zhongshu, Li, Gallagher, Kevin P., and Mauzerall, Denise L. (2021, October 15). Financing Carbon Lock-in in Developing Countries: Bilateral Financing for Power Generation Technologies from China, Japan, and the United States. *Applied Energy*, 300, 117318.

Chen, Yuan (2013). *Aligning State and Market: China's Approach to Development Finance*. Beijing: Foreign Languages Press.

Chin, Gregory (2010). Remaking the Architecture: The Emerging Powers, Self-Insuring and Regional Insulation. *International Affairs*, 86(3), 693–715.

Chin, Gregory (2012, January). Responding to the Global Financial Crisis: The Evolution of Asian Regionalism and Economic Globalization. *ADBI Working Paper*, (343), Tokyo: Asian Development Bank Institute. www.adb.org/sites/default/files/publication/156197/adbi-wp343.pdf.

Chin, Gregory (2012, fall/winter). Two-Way Socialization: China, the World Bank, and Hegemonic Weakening. *The Brown Journal of World Affairs*, 19(1), 211–230.

Chin, Gregory (2014). The BRICS-led Development Bank. *Global Policy*, 5(3), 366–373. https://onlinelibrary.wiley.com/doi/abs/10.1111/1758-5899.

Chin, Gregory (2015). China and the World Bank: The Long Decade. In Freeman, Carla (Ed.), *China and Developing Countries*. Cheltenham: Edward Elgar, 169–192.

Chin, Gregory (2017). True Revisionist: China and the Global Monetary System. In deLisle, J. and Goldstein, A. (Eds.), *China's Global Engagement: Cooperation, Conflict, and Influence in the 21st Century*. Washington, DC: Brookings Institution Press, 35–66.

Chin, Gregory (2019). The Asian Infrastructure Investment Bank as New Multilateralism. *Global Policy*, *10*(4), 569–581.

Chin, Gregory. (2023). China and the United Nations Secretariat: A Mutual Infuencing Game. In Stiles, K. and Oestreich, J. (Eds.), *Global Institutions in a Time of Power Transition: Governing Turbulence*. Cheleanham: Edward Elgar, 41–60.

Chin, Gregory. (2024). The Evolution of New Development Bank. *Global Policy*, 15(2), 368–382. https://onlinelibrary.wiley.com/doi/10.1111/1758-5899.13399.

Chin, Gregory and Helleiner, Eric (2008). China as a Creditor: A Rising Financial Power? *Journal of International Affairs*, 62(1), 87–102.

Chin, Gregory and Gallagher, Kevin (2019, January). Coordinated Credit Spaces: The Globalization of Chinese Development Finance. *Development and Change*.

Chin, Gregory and Thakur, Ramesh (2010). Will China Change the Rules of World Order. *Washington Quarterly*, *33*(4), 119–138.

Chin, Gregory and Stubbs Richard (2011). China, Regional Institution-Building and the China-ASEAN Free Trade Area. *Review of International Political Economy*, *18*(3), 277–298.

China Development Bank (CDB) (2016). Annual Report. *China Development Bank*. www.cdb.com.cn/English/bgxz/ndbg/.

China Export Import (CHEXIM) (2012). Annual Report. http://english.exim bank.gov.cn/News/AnnualR/2012/201807/P020180718670664432446.pdf.

Clift, Ben. (2018) *The IMF and the Politics of Austerity in the Wake of the Global Financial Crisis*. Oxford: Oxford University Press.

Cohen, Benjamin (1998). *The Geography of Money*. Ithaca: Cornell University Press.

Cohen, Benjamin (2007). *Global Monetary Governance*. London: Routledge.

Cohen, Benjamin (2008). The International Monetary System: Diffusion and Ambiguity. *International Affairs*, *84*(3), 455–470.

Cox, Robert W. (1987). *Production, Power*, and *World Order: Social Forces in the Making of History*. New York: Columbia University Press.

Cox, Robert W., and Schechter, Michael (2002). *The Political Economy of a Plural World*. London: Routledge.

Devereaux, C. (2015). *Argentina Said to Secure $400 Million More in China FX Swap*. Bloomberg Business.

Dreher, Axel ; Fuchs, Andreas ; Parks, Bradley ; Strange, Austin ; and Tierney, Michael J. (2022). *Banking on Beijing: The Aims and Impacts of China's Overseas Development Program*. Cambridge: Cambridge University Press.

Dreher, Axel ; Fuchs, Andreas ; Parks, Bradley ; Strange, Austin ; and Tierney, Michael (2021). "Aid, China, and Growth: Evidence from a New Global Development Finance Dataset. *American Economic Journal*. www.aeaweb.org/articles?id=10.1257/pol.20180631.

Drezner, Daniel (2014). *The System Worked*. New York: Oxford University Press.

Drezner, Daniel (2007a). The New New World Order. *Foreign Affairs*, 86(2), 34–46.

Drezner, Daniel (2007b). *All Politics Is Global*. Princeton: Princeton University Press.

Economy, Elizabeth (2004). *The River Runs Black: The Environmental Challenge to China's Future*. Ithaca: Cornell University Press.

Edwards, T. (2015, May 21). *Mongolia Leans on China as It Waits for Cooper Mine-led Revival*. Reuters.

Eichengreen, Barry (2019). *Globalizing Capital: A History of the International Monetary System*. 3rd ed. Princeton: Princeton University Press.

Ferdinand, Peter, and Wang, Jue (2013). China and the IMF: From Mimicry toward Pragmatic International Institutional Pluralism. *International Affairs*, 89(4), 895–910.

Finance in Common (2022, October). *Final Communique*. Abidjan. https://financeincommon.org/sites/default/files/2022-10/FICS%202022%20Final%20Communiqu%C3%A9_0.pdf.

Finnemore, Martha, and Sikkink, Kathryn (1998). International Norm Dynamics and Political Change. *International Organization*, 52(4), 887–917.

Friedberg, Aaron (2022). *Getting China Wrong*. Cambridge: Polity.

Foot, Rosemary, and Walter, Andrew (2011). *China, the United States, and Global Order*. Cambridge: Cambridge University Press.

Frieden, Jeffry (2019). Chapter 1. The Political Economy of the Bretton Woods Agreements. In Lamoreaux, Naomi and Shapiro, Ian (Eds.), *The Bretton Woods Agreements: Together with Scholarly Commentaries and Essential Historical Documents*. New Haven: Yale University Press, pp. 21–37.

Galbraith, J. Kenneth (1952). *American Capitalism: The Concept of Countervailing Power*. Boston: Houghton Mifflin Co.

Gallagher, Kevin (2016): The China Triangle: Latin America's China Boom and the Future of the Washington Consensus, London, Oxford University Press.

Gallagher, Kevin P. (2015). *Ruling Capital: Emerging Markets and the Reregulation of Cross-Border Financial Flows*. Ithaca: Cornel University Press.

Gallagher, Kevin P. (2022, October). China to the Rescue? China's Liquidity Finance Should Be Welcomed but Not Gambled with. *China Global South Project*.

Gallagher, Kevin P., and Irwin, Amos (2015). China's Economic Statecraft in Latin America: Evidence from China's Policy Banks. *Pacific Affairs*, *88*(1), 98–121.

Gallagher, Kevin ; Kring, William ; Ray, Rebecca ; et al. (2023). The BRI at Ten: Maximizing the Benefits and Minimizing the Risks of China's Belt and Road Initiative. *Boston University Global Development Policy Center*.

Gao, Haihong (2023, Summer). The Role of China in the International Financial System. *Oxford Review of Economic Policy*, *39*(2), 231–244.

Gao, Henry, Raess, Damian and Zeng, Ka (Eds.) (2023). *China and the WTO*. Cambridge: Cambridge University Press.

Gilpin, Robert (1987). The Political Economy of International Relations. Princeton: Princeton University Press.

Grabel, Ilene (2018). *When Things Don't Fall Apart: Global Financial Governance and Developmental Finance in an Age of Productive Incoherence*. Cambridge, MA: MIT Press.

Grimes, William, and Kring, William (2020). Institutionalizing Financial Cooperation in East Asia: AMRO and the Future of the Chiang Mai Initiative Multilateralization. *Global Governance*, *26*, 428–448.

Gregory Shaffer and Henry Gao (2018). China's Rise: How It Took on the U.S. at the WTO. *University of Illinois Law Review*, *1*, 116–184.

Guo, Gallagher, and Zhang (2022). Key Pathways on a Green and Low-Carbon BRI. *China Council for International Cooperation on Environment and Development*. Beijing: Chinese Ministry of Ecology and Environment.

Helleiner, Eric (1994). *States and the Re-emergence of Global Finance*. Ithaca: Cornell University Press.

Helleiner, Eric (2014). *The Status Quo Crisis: Global Financial Governance after the 2008 Meltdown*. New York: Oxford University Press.

Helleiner, Eric (2014b). *Forgotten Foundations of Bretton Woods: International Development and the Making of the Postwar Order*. Ithaca: Cornell University Press.

Helleiner, Eric (2014c). The Evolution of the International Monetary and Financial System, in Global Political Economy. In Ravenhill, John (Ed.), *Global Political Economy*. Oxford: Oxford University Press, 213–240.

Helleiner, Eric (2015). The Future of the Euro in a Global Monetary Context. In Matthijs, Matthias and Blyth, Mark (Eds.), *The Future of the Euro*. Oxford: Oxford University Press, 233–248.

Helleiner, Eric (2019). Multilateral Development Finance in Non-western Thought: From before Bretton Woods to beyond. *Development and Change*, *50*, 144–163.

Helleiner, Eric, and Momani, Bessma (2014). The Hidden History of China and the IMF. In Helleiner, Eric, and Kirshner, Jonathan (Eds.), *The Great Wall of Money: Power and Politics in China's International Monetary Relations*. Ithaca: Cornell University Press, 45–70.

Henning, C. Randall (2019). Regime Complexity and the Organizations of Crisis and Development Finance. *Development and Change*, 50(1), 24–45.

Hernandez, Diego (2017). Are "New" Donors Challenging World Bank Conditionality? *World Development 96*, 529–549.

Hirschman, Albert (1945). *National Power and the Structure of Foreign Trade*. Berkeley: University of California Press.

Hirschman, Albert (1970). *Exit, Voice, and Loyalty: Responses to Decline in Firms, Organizations, and States*. Cambridge, MA: Harvard University Press.

Hofman, Bert, and Srinivas, P. S. (2024). New Development Bank's Role in the Global Financial Architecture. *Global Policy*, 15(2), 451–457.

Hu, Angang (2004, May). *Development, Cooperation, Mutual Beneficiary, and Win-Win for All Parties*. Chinese Academy of Sciences/Tsinghua University, Center for China Study.

Hu, Angang, and Wang, Shaoguang. (1999). *The Political Economy of Uneven Development: The Case of China*. New York: M.E. Sharpe.

Humphrey, Christopher, and Chen, Yunnan (2021). *China in the Multilateral Development Banks: Evolving Strategies of a New Power* (Report). London: ODI.

Humphrey, Chris (2022). *Financing the Future: Multilateral Development Banks in the Changing World Order*. London: Oxford University Press.

Humphrey, Christopher (2023). *Financing the Future*. New York: Oxford University Press.

Ikenberry, John and Inoguchi, Takashi (2007). Introduction. In John Ikenberry and Takashi Inoguchi (Eds.), *The Uses of Institutions*. Basingstoke: Palgrave.

Imbert, Fred (2019, April 11). World Bank President David Malpass says there is too much debt in the world. *CNBC*. www.cnbc.com/2019/04/11/world-bank-president-david-malpass-says-china-has-too-much-debt.html.

IMF (2012). Peoples Republic of China: 2012 Article IV Consultation. IMF Country Report No.12/195. www.imf.org/external/pubs/ft/scr/2012/cr12195.pdf.

IMF (2016). *IMF Country Report No.16/319 – Ukraine*. Washington, DC: International Monetary Fund.

International Monetary Fund (IMF) (1996). People's Republic of China Accepts Article VIII Obligations. *IMF Press Release 58*(96), Washington, D.C.

References

International Monetary Fund (IMF) (1998). Statement by Mr. Dai Xianglong, Governor of the People's Bank of China, at the 1998 Annual Meeting of the International Monetary Fund and the World Bank. *IMF Press Release* 14, Washington, D.C.

International Monetary Fund (IMF) (1999, September 26). Statement by Mr. Dai Xianglong, Governor, People's Bank of China, at the Fifty-Third Meeting of the Interim Committee of the Board of Governors of the International Monetary System, IMF, Washington, DC, www.imf.org/external/am/1999/icstate/chn.htm.

International Monetary Fund (IMF) (1999, September 28–30). Statement by Xiang Huaicheng, Governor of the Bank for the People's Republic of China at the Joint Discussion, Board of Governors of the World Bank Group and IMF, 1999 Annual Meetings, Press Release 15, Washington, DC, www.imf.org/external/am/1999/speeches/pr15cne.pdf

International Monetary Fund (IMF) (2006). IMF Article IV Consultation for the People's Republic of China, Washington, DC, www.imf.org/external/pubs/ft/scr/2006/cr06394.pdf.

International Monetary Fund (IMF) (2007, June 21). Public Information Notice: IMF Executive Board Adopts New Decision on Bilateral Surveillance Over Members' Policies, PIN No. 07/69. www.imf.org/en/News/Articles/2015/09/28/04/53/pn0769#:~:text=On%20June%2015%2C%202007%2C%20the,repealing%20and%20replacing%20that%20Decision.

International Monetary Fund (IMF) (2009, November). Report on the Technical Assistance Evaluation Mission to the People's Republic of China, Washington, D.C. www.imf.org/external/np/pp/eng/2009/111109.pdf.

International Monetary Fund (IMF) (2010a, October 26). Review of the Method of Valuation of the SDR, prepared by the Finance Department in consultation with the Legal and other departments. www.imf.org/external/np/pp/eng/2010/102610.pdf.

International Monetary Fund (IMF) (2010b, November 17). Public Information Notice: IMF Executive Board Completes the 2010 Review of SDR Valuation. www.imf.org/en/News/Articles/2015/09/28/04/53/pn10149.

International Monetary Fund (IMF) (2011). IMF Article IV Consultation for the People's Republic of China, *IMF Country Report* 11/*192*(11), Washington, DC. www.imf.org/external/pubs/ft/scr/2011/cr11192.pdf.

International Monetary Fund (IMF) (2017, May 16). IMF Managing Director Meets Chinese Leadership and Participates in the Belt and Road Forum in Beijing. *IMF Press Release 175*(17). www.imf.org/en/News/Articles/2017/05/16/PR17175-IMF-Managing-Director-Meets-Chinese-Leadership-and-Participates-in-Belt-and-Road-Forum.

International Monetary Fund (IMF) (2018, April 12). A Joint People's Bank of China–International Monetary Fund High-Level Conference on the Belt and Road Initiative (BRI). *IMF Conference.* www.imf.org/en/News/Seminars/Conferences/2018/03/27/BJ-BRI.

International Monetary Fund (IMF) (2019, April 26). BRI 2.0: Stronger Frameworks in the New Phase of Belt and Road, speech by Christine Lagarde, IMF Managing Director. www.imf.org/en/News/Articles/2019/04/25/sp042619-stronger-frameworks-in-the-new-phase-of-belt-and-road.

International Monetary Fund (IMF) (2021). China: Transactions with the Fund from May 1, 1984, to February 29, 2024, *IMF.* www.imf.org/external/np/fin/tad/extrans1.aspx?memberKey1=180andendDate=2099-12-31andfinposition_flag=YES.

International Monetary Fund (IMF) (2021a). China: History of Lending Commitments as of December 31, 2015. www.imf.org/external/np/fin/tad/extarr2.aspx?memberKey1=180anddate1key=2015-12-31.

International Monetary Fund (IMF) (2021b). China: Transactions with the Fund from May 1, 1984, to April 30, 2023. www.imf.org/external/np/fin/tad/extrans1.aspx?memberKey1=180andendDate=2099-12-31andfinposition_flag=YES.

International Monetary Fund (IMF) (2022). IMF Institute Training at the China-IMF Capacity Development Center (CICDC), Beijing, China. IMF Institute. www.imf.org/en/Capacity-Development/Training/ICDTC/Schedule/CT.

Jacobson, Harold, and Oksenberg, Michel (1990). *China's Participation in the IMF, the World Bank, and GATT: Toward a Global Economic Order.* Ann Arbor: University of Michigan Press.

Jalles, Joao Tovar, Kiendrebeogo, Youssouf, Lam, Waikei, and Piazza, Roberto (2023). Revisiting Countercyclicality in Fiscal Policy. *IMF Working Paper*, 2023/098. www.elibrary.imf.org/view/journals/001/2023/089/article-A001-en.xml.

James, Harold (2012). "The Multiple Contexts of Bretton Woods." *Oxford Review of Economic Policy, 28*(3), 411–430.

Johnson, Alastair Iain (2008). *Social States: China in International Institutions, 1980–2000.* Princeton: Princeton University Press.

Jones, Bruce (2014). *Still Ours to Lead: America, Rising Powers, and the Tension Between Rivalry and Restraint.* Washington, DC: Brookings Institution Press.

Kaplan, Stephen B. (2021). *Globalizing Patient Capital: The Political Economy of Chinese Finance in the Americas.* Cambridge: Cambridge University Press.

Kastner, Scott; Pearson, Margaret; and Rector, Chad (2019). *China's Strategic Multilateralism: Investing in Global Governance*. Cambridge: Cambridge University Press.

Kastner, Scott, Pearson, Margaret, and Rector, Chad (2020). "China and Global Governance." *Global Policy*, 11(1), 164–169. https://onlinelibrary.wiley.com/doi/abs/10.1111/1758-5899.12772?campaign=wolearlyview.

Kent, Ann (2007). *Beyond Compliance: China, International Organizations, and Global Security*. Stanford: Stanford University Press.

Keohane, Robert (1984). Chapter 4. In Robert Keohane (ed.), *After Hegemony: Cooperation and Discord in* the *World Political Economy*. Princeton: Princeton University Press, 49–64.

Khan, Azizur Rahman, and Riskin, Carl (2001). *Inequality and Poverty in China in the Age of Globalization*. New York: Oxford University Press.

Kindleberger, C. P. (1973). *The World in Depression, 1929–1939*. Berkeley: University of California Press.

Kirshner, Jonathan. (2014) *American Power after the Financial Crisis*. Ithaca: Cornell University Press.

Kissinger, Henry A. (2010). Power Shifts. *Survival*, 52(6), 205–212.

Kong, Bo, and Gallagher, Kevin P. (2017, November 2). Globalizing Chinese Energy Finance: The Role of Policy Banks. *Journal of Contemporary China*, 26(108), 834–851.

Kong. Bo, and Gallagher, Kevin (2020). "Chinese Development Finance for Solar and Wind Power Abroad", Boston University, Global Development Policy Center, *GCI Working Paper,* 009/01. www.bu.edu/gdp/files/2020/02/WP9-Kong-Bo-inc_abstract.pdf.

Kristen Hopewell (2016). *Breaking the WTO*. Stanford: Stanford University Press.

Kupchan, Charles (2012). *No One's World: The West, the Rising Rest, and the Coming Global Turn*. New York: Oxford University Press.

Lardy, Nicholas (1992). *Foreign Trade and Economic Reform in China, 1978–1990*. Cambridge: Cambridge University Press.

Lardy, Nicholas (1998). *China's Unfinished Economic Revolution*. Washington, DC: Brookings Institution Press.

Lardy, Nicholas (1999). China and the International Financial System. In Economy, Elizabeth, and Oksenberg, Michel (Eds.), *China Joins the World*. New York: Council on Foreign Relations Press, 206–230.

Lawder, David (2023). World Bank Chief Sees $100 Billion-Plus Lending Boost from Capital Moves. *Reuters*, 26 September. www.reuters.com/business/finance/banga-says-country-contributions-could-boost-world-bank-lending-capacity-2023-09-26/.

Layne, Christopher (2018). The US-China Power Shift and the End of the Pax Americana. *International Affairs*, *94*(1), 89–111.

Lee, Ching Kwan (1998). *Gender and the South China Miracle: Two Worlds of Factory Women*. Berkeley: University of California Press.

Li, Zhongshu, Gallagher, Kevin, Chen, Xu, Yuan, Jiahai, and Mauzerall, Denise L. (2022, April 1). "Pushing Out or Pulling In? The Determinants of Chinese Energy Finance in Developing Countries." *Energy Research and Social Science, 86*.

Lichtenstein, Natalie (2018). *A Comparative Guide to the Asian Infrastructure Investment Bank*. New York: Oxford University Press.

Lin, Paul T. K. (1981). The People's Republic of China and the New International Economic Order. In Jorge Lozoya and A. K. Bhattacharya (Eds.), *Asia and the New International Economic Order*. New York: Pergamon Press, pp. 39–52.

Liu, Jianchao (2024). The Future of China and US Relations. Council on Foreign Relations. www.youtube.com/watch?v=2-pfr5xa6yM.

Liu, K. (2021). Statement by H.E. Ken Liu, Minister of Finance, on behalf of the People's Republic of China at the 104th Meeting of the De-velopment Committee. *The World Bank Group*, Washington, DC.

Maasdorp, Leslie. (2015). What Is "New" about the New Development Bank. *World Economic Forum*, 26 August, www.weforum.org/stories/2015/08/what-is-new-about-the-new-development-bank/.

Maasdorp, Leslie. (2019). BRICS' New Bank Turns Four: What Has It Achieved? *World Economic Forum*, 20 September, www.weforum.org/stories/2019/09/brics-new-development-bank-four-sustainability/.

Maier, Charles S. (1977). The Politics of Productivity: Foundations of American International Economic Policy after World War II, International Organization, Cambridge University Press, 31(4), 607–633, October.

Malkin, Anton, and Momani, Bessma (2019). From Activism to Status Quo: The Convergence of State and Institutional Preferences in China's Relationship with the IMF. In Zeng, Ka (Ed.), *Handbook on the International Political Economy of China*. Cheltenham: Edward Elgar, 298–311.

Mandon, Pierre, and Woldemichael, Martha Tesfaye (2023). Has Chinese Aid Benefited Recipient Countries? Evidence from a Meta-Regression Analysis. *World Development 166*.

Martinot, Eric (2001). World Bank Energy Projects in China: Influences on Environmental Protection. *Energy Policy*, *29*(8), 581–594.

McDowell, Daniel (2019). The (Ineffective) Financial Statecraft of China's Bilateral Swap Agreements. *Development and Change*, *50*(1), 122–143.

Ministry of Finance of the People's Republic of China (Ministry of Finance) (2019, April 25). Debt Sustainability Framework for Participating Countries in the Belt and Road Initiative. http://m.mof.gov.cn/czxw/201904/P020190425513990982189.pdf.

Ministry of Foreign Affairs of the People's Republic of China (2000, November 15). China and the International Monetary Fund (IMF). www.fmprc.gov.cn/mfa_eng/wjb_663304/zzjg_663340/gjs_665170/gjzzyhy_665174/2594_665176/2600_665188/200011/t20001115_598031.html.

Morris, Scott (2023). Development Finance Cooperation amidst Great Power Competition: What Role for the World Bank? *Oxford Review of Economic Policy*, 39, 379–388.

Morris, Scott, and Portelance, Gailyn (2019). Examining World Bank Lending to China: Graduation or Modulation? *CGD Policy Paper*. Washington, DC: Center for Global Development.

Morris, Scott ; Rockafellow, Rowan ; and Rose, Sarah (2021). Mapping China's Multilateralism: A Data Survey of China's Participation in Multilateral Development Institutions and Funds. *CGD Policy Paper 241*. Washington, DC: Center for Global Development.

Moses, Oyintarelado, and Zhu, Keren (2022). *The Belt and Road Initiative and the Partnership for Global Infrastructure and Investment*. Boston: Boston University Global Development Policy Center.

New Development Bank. (2022). *General Strategy, 2022–2026*. www.ndb.int/about-ndb/general-strategy/.

Nolan, Peter (2001). *China and the Global Economy: National Champions, Industrial Policy, and the Big Business Revolution*. Basingstoke: Palgrave Macmillan.

Nolan, Peter (2021). *China in the Asian Financial Crisis*. London: Routledge.

Patey, Luke (2017). "China Made Mauricio Macri a Deal He Couldn't Refuse." *Foreign Policy*, 24 January, https://foreignpolicy.com/2017/01/24/china-made-mauricio-macri-a-deal-he-couldnt-refuse/.

Pearson, Margaret (1999). The Major Multilateral Economic Institutions Engage China. In Johnston, Alastair Iain, and Ross, Robert (Eds.), *Engaging China*. New York: Routledge, 207–234.

Pearson, Margaret. (2006). China in Geneva: Lessons from China's Early Years in the World Trade Organization. In Johnston, A. I. and Ross, R. S. (Eds.), *New Directions in the Study of China's Foreign Policy*. Stanford: Stanford University Press, 242–275.

Peking University and AFD (2023). 2023 Q2 Update of the Global Database on PDBs and DFIs. Public Development Banks and Development Financing

Institutions Database. www.dfidatabase.pku.edu.cn/News/181602722aa64a97af3ab32c656fcc99.htm.

People's Bank of China (1996). Regulations on the Management of the Settlement, Sale, and Purchase of Foreign Exchange.

Rana, S. (2013). *Money Out of Nowhere*. The Express Tribune.

Rappeport, Alan (2019). U.S. Objects to World Bank's Lending Plans for China. *New York Times*, December 5. www.nytimes.com/2019/12/05/business/us-china-world-bank.html.

Reuters (2019, October 29). China Pushes Back against Criticism of Its Belt and Road Lending, Voice of America. www.voanews.com/a/economy-business_china-pushes-back-against-criticism-its-belt-and-road-lending/6178503>.html.

Reuters (2014, November 17). Argentina Receives Second Currency Swap from China. www.reuters.com/article/markets/us/argentina-receives-second-currency-swap-from-china-idUSL2N0T72RD/#:~:text=BUENOS%20AIRES%2C%20Nov%2017%20(Reuters,up%20its%20ailing%20foreign%20reserves.

Reuters (2016, November 8). Egypt Has Secured $6 Billion Bilateral Financing Required for IMF Loan.

Riskin, Carl. (1987). *China's Political Economy: The Quest for Development Since 1949*. New York: Oxford University Press.

Roberts, Cynthia; Armijo, Leslie Elliott; and Katada, Saori (2018). *The BRICS and Collective Financial Statecraft*. Oxford: Oxford University Press.

Ruggie, John Gerald (1982). International Regimes, Transactions, and Change: Embedded Liberalism in the Postwar Economic Order. *International Organization*, 36(2), 379–415.

Sanderson, Henry, and Forsythe, Michael (2012). *China's Superbank: Debt, Oil and Influence – How China Development Bank Is Rewriting the Rules of Finance*. New York: Bloomberg.

Shaffer, Gregory, and Gao, Henry. (2018). China Rise: How It Took on the U.S. at the WTO. *University of Illinois Law Review*, 1, 115–184.

Shambaugh, David. (2013). *China Goes Global: The Partial Power*. New York: Oxford University Press.

Solinger, Dorothy (1999). *Contesting Citizenship in Urban China: Peasant Migrants, the State, and the Logic of the Market*. Berkeley: University of California Press.

Stott, Michael (2022, September 26). Inter-American Development Bank votes to oust Donald Trump-era president. *Financial Times*, www.ft.com/content/6745c027-457a-4cae-a7d6-7f7d0e00b009.

Strange, Susan (1976). *International Monetary Relations (International Economic Relations of the Western World, 1959–1971)*. Oxford: Oxford University Press.

Strange, Susan (1987). The Persistent Myth of Lost Hegemony. *International Organization, 41*(4), 551–574.

Strange, Susan (1988). *States and Markets*. London: Pinter.

Stubbs, Thomas; Kring, William; Laskaridis, Christina; Kentikelenis, Alexander; and Gallagher, Kevin (2021). Whatever It Takes? The Global Financial Safety Net, Covid-19, and Developing Countries. *World Development, 137*, 105171.

Sundquist, James. (2021, February 15). Bailouts from Beijing How China Functions as an Alternative to the IMF. *Boston University Global Development Policy Working Paper*. Boston University Global Development Policy Center.

Truman, Edwin (2018). China, the United States, and Damage to the IMF. *PIIE.com*, September 4, www.piie.com/blogs/realtime-economic-issues-watch/china-united-states-and-damage-imf.

Walter, Carl and Howie, Faser (2012). *Red Capitalism*. Singapore: Wiley.

Wang, Jue (2018). China-IMF Collaboration: Toward the Leadership in Global Monetary Governance. *China Political Science Review, 3*, 62–80.

Wang, Jue, and Sampson, Michael. (2022, Winter). China's Multi-Front Institutional Strategies in International Development Finance. *The Chinese Journal of International Politics, 15*(4), 374–394.

Wilson, Elliot (2020). Asia: Could COVID-19 be the Making of the AIIB? *Euromoney*, 22 April. www.euromoney.com/article/b1l9lyrb8ztsqc/asia-could-covid-19-be-the-making-of-the-aiib.

World Bank (2000, April 17). Statement by Mr. Jin Liqun, Vice Minister of Finance, People's Republic of China, 61st Meeting of the Development Committee. World Bank.

World Bank (2005). World Bank President Paul Wolfowitz at his Medai Conference Marking the End of His Six Day Trip to China, http://siteresources.worldbank.org/NEWS/Resources/101805-PWChinaClose.mp3. Accessed 21 May 2014.

World Bank (2016, August 31). World Bank Successfully Prices Oversubscribed Landmark SDR-Denominated Bond in China. *World Bank Press Release*. www.worldbank.org/en/news/press-release/2016/08/31/world-bank-successfully-prices-oversubscribed-landmark-sdr-denominated-bond-in-china#:~:text=The%20SDR%20Denominated%20Bonds%20were,equivalent%20to%20USD%202.8%20billion).

World Bank (2019). China – Country Partnership Framework for the Period FY20202–2025. *World Bank – Documents and Reports*. https://documents.worldbank.org/en/publication/documents-reports/documentdetail/902781575573489712/china-country-partnership-framework-for-the-period-fy2020-2025.

World Bank (2019). Belt and Road Economics: Opportunities and Risks of Transport Corridors. Washington, DC: World Bank.

World Bank (2023, February 7). World Bank Issues Sustainable Development Bond While Highlighting the Importance of Sustainable Cities in Eliminating Poverty and Boosting Shared Prosperity. *World Bank Press Release.* www.worldbank.org/en/news/press-release/2023/02/07/world-bank-issues-sustainable-development-bond-while-highlighting-importance-of-sustainable-cities-in-eliminating-povert.

World Bank and State Environmental Protection Agency (2007). The Cost of Pollution in China. Washington and Beijing: World Bank. https://documents1.worldbank.org/curated/en/782171468027560055/pdf/392360CHA0Cost1of1Pollution01PUBLIC1.pdf.

World Bank and the Development Research Center of the State Council, the People's Republic of China (2022). Four Decades of Poverty Reduction in China: Drivers, Insights for the World, and the Way Ahead. Washington, DC: World Bank.

Xiang, Huaicheng (1999, September 28). Statement by the Hon. Xiang Huaicheng, Governor of the Bank of the People's Republic of China, at the Joint Annual Discussion. *International Monetary Fund, Press Release 15.* Washington, DC, www.imf.org/external/am/1999/speeches/pr15cne.pdf.

Xinhua (2016, December 8). Turkey, China Conclude First Lira-Yuan Swap Deal.

Yang, Hongbo B., Simmons, Alexander, Ray, Rebecca, et al., (2021, November). Risks to Global Biodiversity and Indigenous Lands from China's Overseas Development Finance. *Nature Ecology and Evolution,* 5(11), 1520–1529.

Ye, Min (2020). *The Belt, Road, and beyond.* Cambridge: Cambridge University Press.

Zeitz, Alexandra (2021). Emulate or Differentiate? *Review of International Organization,* 16, 265–292.

Zeng, Ka, and Liang, Wei (2013). *China and Global Trade Governance: China's First Decade in the World Trade Organization.* Abingdon: Routledge.

Zhang, Guang (2004). The Determinants of Foreign Aid Allocation across China: The Case of World Bank Loans. *Asian Survey,* 44(5), 691–710.

Zhou, Xiaochuan (2010), Statement by Zhou Xiaochuan, Annual Meetings of the International Monetary Fund, Washington, DC, International Monetary Fund. www.imf.org/external/am/2010/speeches/pr47e.pdf.

Zucker Marques, Marina, and Kring, William (2023, December 12). "Who Will Come to the Rescue? The Inadequacies of the Global Financial Safety Net and Its Impact on Developing Countries. *China Global South Project.* https://chinaglobalsouth.com/?s=William+Kring.

Acknowledgments

The authors would like to thank Ching Kwan Lee for her interest and encouragement in this project for the Global China Series, and Senior Commissioning Editor Lucy Rhymer at Cambridge University Press. Gregory Chin and Kevin Gallagher wish to thank each of the staff, fellows, and faculty in the Global China Initiative (GCI) and the Boston University Global Development Policy Center. Special thanks go to Maureen Heydt Danlei Liao and Angie Ye for their copyediting and strategic communications related to the volume. This Element is partly a function of our collective learning and efforts at GCI. Kevin Gallagher extends his gratitude to Boston University's Pardee School of Global Studies, while Gregory Chin thanks York University, especially the LA&PS Dean J. J. McMurtry, Associate Deans Ravi de Costa and David Mutimer, and the Department of Politics. We also thank officials of the IMF, BIS, World Bank Group, CAF, ADB, AMRO, AIIB, NDB, the People's Bank of China, China's Ministry of Finance, China's Ministry of Foreign Affairs, Hong Kong Monetary Authority, and central banks and finance ministries around the world for the research interviews. Our thanks to colleagues at the Chinese Academy of Social Sciences, Institute for World Economics and Politics, especially Yu Yongding, Gao Haihong, Zhang Ming, Wang Yongzhong, and Huang Ping at the Institute of European Studies; Justin Yifu Lin, Jiajun Xu, and Wang Yan at the Institute for New Structural Economics at Peking University; and Hu Angang at Tsinghua University. We give special thanks to Eva-Maria Nag, Benjamin J. Cohen, Andrew Cooper, Robert Cox, Joseph Fewsmith, Carla Freeman, Giuseppe Gabusi, William Grimes, Eric Helleiner, Jorge Heine, Jonathan Kirshner, William Kring, Louis Pauly, Margaret Pearson, Wang Yong, Zhu Jiejin, Zhu Tianbiao, and colleagues Manmohan Agarwal, Vinod Agarwal, Chris Alden, Alan Alexandroff, Giovanni Andornino, Agata Antkiewicz, Leslie Armijo, Mark Blyth, Thomas Bernes, Pieter Bottelier, Paul Bowles, Daniel Bradlow, Anna Caffarena, David Carment, Muyang Chen, Yunnan Chen, Chen Zhimin, Ding Yifan, Hugo Dobson, Cinnamon Dornsife, John English, Victor Falkenheim, Bernie Frolic, Min Gao, Randall Germain, Mui Pong Goh, Fumihito Gotoh, Jorn-Carsten Gottwald, Ilene Grabel, Stephan Haggard, Sandra Heep, Sebastian Heilmann, Randall Henning, Patrick Hess, John M. Hobson, Kathryn Hochstetler, Bert Hofman, Kristin Hopewell, Huang Ping, Chris Humphrey, Yang Jiang, Yijia Jing, Alistair Iain Johnson, Juliet Johnson, Bruce Jutzi,

Miles Kahler, Sawar Kashmeri, Scott Kennedy, John Kirton, Madeline Koch, Daniel Koldyk, Cheng-Chwee Kuik, David Lampton, Yaechan Lee, Garth le Pere, Dries Lesage, Li Mingjiang, Vic Li, Li Wei, Wei Liang, John Lipsky, Natalie Lichtenstein, Zongyuan Zoe Liu, Sonny Lo, Anton Malkin, Magalie Masamba, Alvaro Mendez, Bessma Momani, Riann Meyer, Jim O'Neill, Suresh Nanwani, Jeremy Paltiel, Pang Zhongying, Michaela Papa, Anthony Payne, T. J. Pempel, Sergei Plekhanov, Cyril Prinsloo, Cintia Quiliconi, John Ravenhill, Rebecca Ray, Andrew Schrumm, David Shambaugh, Timothy Shaw, Kurtis Simpson, Injoo Sohn, P. S. Srinivas, Barbara Stallings, Austin Strange, Richard Stubbs, Su Changhe, Paola Subacchi, Christopher Swarat, Heiwai Tang, Ramesh Thakur, Yves Tiberghien, Diana Tussie, Robert Wade, Andrew Walter, Hongying Wang, Jue Wang, Wang Zaibang, Karl Yan, Min Ye, Zha Daojiong, and Marina Zucker-Marques. This work could not have been conducted without the generous support of the Carnegie Corporation of New York, the Rockefeller Brothers Fund, the Charles Stewart Mott Foundation, the Gates Foundation, and others who support our work at the Global China Initiative.

Cambridge Elements

Global China

Ching Kwan Lee
University of California-Los Angeles

Ching Kwan Lee is professor of sociology at the University of California-Los Angeles. Her scholarly interests include political sociology, popular protests, labor, development, political economy, comparative ethnography, China, Hong Kong, East Asia and the Global South. She is the author of three multiple award-winning monographs on contemporary China: Gender and the South China Miracle: Two Worlds of Factory Women (1998), Against the Law: Labor Protests in China's Rustbelt and Sunbelt (2007), and The Specter of Global China: Politics, Labor and Foreign Investment in Africa (2017). Her co-edited volumes include Take Back Our Future: an Eventful Sociology of Hong Kong's Umbrella Movement (2019) and The Social Question in the 21st Century: A Global View (2019).

About the Series

The Cambridge Elements series Global China showcases thematic, region- or country-specific studies on China's multifaceted global engagements and impacts. Each title, written by a leading scholar of the subject matter at hand, combines a succinct, comprehensive and up-to-date overview of the debates in the scholarly literature with original analysis and a clear argument. Featuring cutting edge scholarship on arguably one of the most important and controversial developments in the 21st century, the Global China Elements series will advance a new direction of China scholarship that expands China Studies beyond China's territorial boundaries.

Cambridge Elements

Global China

Elements in the Series

Chinese Soft Power
Maria Repnikova

Clash of Empires: From 'Chimerica' to the 'New Cold War'
Ho-fung Hung

The Hong Kong-China Nexus: A Brief History
John Carroll

Global China as Method
Ivan Franceschini and Nicholas Loubere

Hong Kong: Global China's Restive Frontier
Ching Kwan Lee

China and Global Food Security
Shaohua Zhan

China in Global Health: Past and Present
Mary Augusta Brazelton

Chinese Global Infrastructure
Austin Strange

Global China's Shadow Exchange
Tak-Wing Ngo

Global Civil Society and China
Anthony J. Spires

China and the Global Economic Order
Gregory T. Chin and Kevin P. Gallagher

A full series listing is available at: www.cambridge.org/EGLC

For EU product safety concerns, contact us at Calle de José Abascal, 56–1°,
28003 Madrid, Spain or eugpsr@cambridge.org.

www.ingramcontent.com/pod-product-compliance
Lightning Source LLC
LaVergne TN
LVHW011852060526
838200LV00054B/4291